Spoken American English

最新改訂版
アメリカ口語教本
入門用

Introductory Course
William L. Clark

KENKYUSHA

Copyright © 1959, 1962, 1972, 1984, 2006 by WILLIAM L. CLARK
All rights reserved according to international law. This book or any parts thereof may not be reproduced in any form without written permission of the author.

First Edition Dec. 1959
Revised Edition Jan. 1962
Third Edition Nov. 1972
Fourth Edition April 1984
Fifth Edition Oct. 2006

ブックデザイン　　　　　Malpu Design（清水良洋 + 佐野佳子）
イラスト・巻末チャート　　伊藤直子

CONTENTS

PREFACE（序　文）.. iv
PREFACE TO THE NEW EDITION（最新改訂版序文）............... vi
SOME SUGGESTIONS TO THE STUDENT（学習者のための指針）... viii
LIST OF PHONETIC SYMBOLS（発音記号表）....................... x

LESSONS:

One	HOW DO YOU DO?（はじめまして）................................	1
Two	MAY I ASK A QUESTION?（お尋ねしてもよろしいですか）....	15
Three	A SPOON AND SOME ICE CREAM（スプーンとアイスクリーム）..	37
Four	WHAT DID YOU DO TODAY?（今日は何をしましたか）......	55
Five	WHAT'S YOUR NAME?（お名前は）.................................	72
Six	A LOOK INTO THE FUTURE（将来の見通し）.......................	94
Seven	HOW HAVE YOU BEEN?（どうしていましたか）.................	110
Eight	GOING TO THE MOVIES（映画を見に行く）.........................	129
Nine	I WONDER WHO INVENTED TELEVISION（だれがテレビを発明したのでしょう）...	147
Ten	I WONDER WHAT HE BOUGHT（彼は何を買ったのでしょう）..	163

CHARTS（図　表）... 巻末

PREFACE（序　文）

This text, the first in a series of four books, is intended for Japanese students who have already completed several years of English instruction in junior and senior high schools. It is supposed that the student will have a certain basic knowledge of English which is quite strong in some points and quite weak in others. This book aims to help the student strengthen weak points and attain fluency and flexibility in certain basic requirements.

Experience in the classroom and comparison of Japanese and English reveal that the problems of English nouns, their number, their determiners, and their modification present enormous difficulties to the Japanese student. Question patterns, too, are a source of much trouble. Accordingly, these two problems are given major attention in this book.

The dialogue in each lesson should be drilled using mim-mem (mimic and memorize). In mim-mem the instructor presents the material in the text, speaking at normal conversational speed and without varying his delivery for any given sentence. The class repeats after the instructor sentence by sentence, if necessary phrase by phrase, until satisfactory pronunciation has been attained. This does not mean that the student must sound exactly like a native speaker; but pronunciation should be natural enough that misunderstanding does not occur. Mim-mem can be done in unison, by rows, and by individuals. During mim-mem books should be closed. This basic oral drill will provide the student with a good memorized background from which to proceed to the more involved problem of attaining fluency and flexibility. Every class hour should be begun with mim-mem of the dialogue at hand as well as review mim-mem of dialogues previously studied. The explanatory material of *Section III* of each lesson should be assigned for study at home. *Section IV* of each lesson takes up specific pronunciation problems, giving basic explanation and drill. Too much time, however, should not be spent on isolated practice of this kind. On the spot correction during mim-mem and pattern drill (*Section V* of each lesson) is much more effective.

The complete *Spoken American English Series* consists of four titles: *Introductory Course*, *Elementary Course*, *Intermediate Course*, and *Advanced Course*. A two-CD set is included with each textbook.

WILLIAM L. CLARK

PREFACE TO THE NEW EDITION
（最新改訂版序文）

First, we would like to state that it is both an honor and a privilege to be part of the rewriting and updating of the *Spoken American English* series. It was a great joy to revise this excellent textbook by the late author; Mr. William L. Clark. Mr. Clark's insight and concern for helping the Japanese master the English language led to, what we consider to be, one of the finest English language texts on the market. Over many years of teaching, both in the United States and here in Japan, we have encountered hundreds of textbooks. While each text has its own unique and valid approach, we believe that the *Spoken American English* series offers the best application and presentation of "living American English." That is to say this text allows the instructors to teach their students the English which is actually used by the people living in America.

All too often ordinary language textbooks use language that native speakers would NOT use in their daily life. This is where the *Spoken American English* series really shines. In addition to its academically sound language acquisition process and progression, and clear easy to understand explanations of the sometimes tricky grammar points, the *Spoken American English* series provides the learner with realistic, and current Americanisms. This text also skillfully exhibits these useful colloquial expressions in natural communicative formats.

While most language texts have a very short life, Mr. Clark's work has stood the test of time. Over the years, this series has proven itself time and time again. Hailed by Japanese educators, native English teachers and students alike, Mr. Clark's method produces results and helps create good English speakers. One reason for the success of this text is that it addresses and clearly explains the common errors made by many Japanese speakers of English. In addition to language acquisition, the learner will also gain a better grasp of some of the intricacies of present-day American culture.

In this Fifth Edition we added short "Presentations" to help introduce the focal points in each of the dialogues. Also each dialogue was carefully examined and revived to assure that all of the expressions were current and timely. As American English is an ever changing language, certain expressions needed to be changed and some text content needed to be updated. But we did our best to maintain the essence of the original author.

Use this book well and efficiently and you can be confident that your English language ability will increase. At the same time, this text will empower you to use those English skills in "real-world" speaking situations.

In closing, a great thanks is due to all the people who gave so much to this revision.

DANIEL J. WOODS (Yokohama Board of Education)
KOICHI JIN (Emeritus Professor, Tokyo Metropolitan University)
HIROSHI NAKAMURA (Editor / Planning)

SOME SUGGESTIONS TO THE STUDENT
（学習者のための指針）

　英会話の本を読んだからといって英語が話せるようになるとは限りません．流ちょうに話す人，すなわち本国人か英語をマスターした人の発音をまねることによってのみ英語が話せるようになります．もし本当に英語が上手になることを望まれるなら，立派な先生につくか，もしそれが不可能なら，正確な音声教材で勉強しなければなりません．本書を使用されるについて，このことを忘れないでください．

　立派な先生につくか，本書付属の CD を使って，本書の勉強を始めてください．まず最初に *Section II* の対話を注意深く聞いてから各課にはいってください．皆さんにとって，「おかしい」と思われるようなところをよく聞きとってください．というのは，それこそ英語を上手に話すためには，まねていただかなければならない事がらなのですから．たとえば，英語には日本語のような規則的強勢がないことに気づくでしょう．英語の音には loud（大きい），slow（ゆっくり）なものがあり，また soft（小さい），quick（速い）なものもあります．これに対して日本語では，個々の音は loudness（大きさ），quickness（速さ）の点でだいたい等しいのです．英語の強勢は日本語のそれと比較したとき，非常に「おかしく」聞こえるでしょう．皆さんは，自分の英語の音を同じように「おかしく」聞こえるようにしなければなりません．もし皆さんの英語が自分に「自然に」聞こえるようでしたら，おそらく英米人にはおかしく聞こえるでしょう．

　対話を数回聞いてから，流ちょうに，自然に発音できるまで CD か，あるいは先生についてくりかえしてください．初めのうちは，なかなかむずかしく，その上完全にはいかないかもしれませんが，そのうちに上達するはずです．各課の *Section IV* にはその課で学ぶ発音についての練習と説明があります．

　Practice makes perfect.（練習は完全をつくる[習うより慣れよ]）という諺があります．しかし，もしまちがった事がら，あるいはまちがった方法で練習しますと，皆さんの英語はよくなるどころか，かえってますます悪くなるでしょう．この昔からの諺は Perfect practice makes perfect.（完全な練習は完

SOME SUGGESTIONS TO THE STUDENT

全をつくる)と変えなければなりません．完全になるよう心がけながら毎日練習してください．最初に各課の *Section II* を練習し，つぎに英語の流ちょうさ，適応性を発達させるための種々の練習問題となる *Section V* をやってください．急いではいけません．注意深く，合理的に練習してください．そうすれば1日1日英語がうまくなっていることに気づかれるでしょう．

　各課には練習についてのくわしい指示があります．さらに各課の *Section III* は，それぞれの例文によって，その課の主要点の説明となっています．*Section V* の練習問題を始める前に *Section III* をよく勉強してください．

　上のような指示に従って本書を注意深く勉強すれば，2, 3か月で本シリーズの次の巻 *Elementary Course*（初級用）に進むことができます．さらに *Intermediate Course*（中級用），*Advanced Course*（上級用）へとつづいています．4巻の全コースを上記の要点に従って慎重に勉強すれば，皆さんは日常生活においていつでも，英語を使う人々に会えば友だちになり，お互いにスムーズに話しあえるようになれるでしょう．

W. L. クラーク

LIST OF PHONETIC SYMBOLS [発音記号表]

VOWELS（母音）

iː	b*ee*
i	b*i*g
e	*e*nd
æ	c*a*t
ə	*a*bout
ʌ[1]	h*u*t
ɚ	cent*er*
ɑ	*o*dd
uː	m*oo*n
u	b*oo*k
ɔ	*a*ll

DIPHTHONGS（二重母音）

ai	*eye*
au	c*ow*
ɔi	b*oy*
ei	f*a*ce
ou	g*o*

CONSONANTS（子音）

b	*b*ed
d	*d*o
ð	*th*is
dʒ	*J*apan
f	*f*an
g	*g*um
h	*h*at
j	*y*es
k	*k*ind
l	*l*ook
m	*m*an
n	*n*ote
ŋ	i*n*k
p	*p*eace
r	*r*adio
s	*s*ea
ʃ	*sh*ip
t	*t*oo
θ	*th*ink
tʃ	*ch*ain
v	*v*ery
w	*w*in
z	*z*oo
ʒ	mea*s*ure

ACCENT（アクセント）

´	primary stress
`	secondary stress

なお，発音記号中 [njuː] のように斜字体になっているものは，省略可能であることを表わしています。

---

1) アメリカ英語では，実際上 [ə] と [ʌ] の音の違いはありません．ですから，アメリカの辞書では，[ʌ] の記号を使わないものが多いわけです．本書では，強勢があるときには [ʌ] を，強勢がないときには [ə] を使うことにします．

LIST OF PHONETIC SYMBOLS

Take special care to distinguish between [i] and [i:]. They are completely different vowel sounds, one *not* being a mere elongation of the other. In this case and in the case of [u] and [u:], [:] does *not* indicate length but unites with the symbols [i] and [u] to form new symbols for phonetically distinct sounds. In all other cases [:] merely indicates a lengthening of the vowel. All pronunciations indicated in the text are American.

[i] と [i:] を区別するよう特に注意してください．一方が他方の長くなった音というだけでなく，この2つは全く違った母音なのです．また [u] と [u:] の場合も同様です．[i] や [u] の次にある [:] 印は長さを示すわけではなく，[i] や [u] といっしょになってそれぞれ別の新しい音を示す記号となるのです．なおここに示す発音はすべてアメリカ式です．

― ● CD について ―
本書には，ネイティブ・スピーカーが吹き込んだ CD が付いています．本書 *Section I* の解説，*Section II* の対話，*Section IV* の発音練習，*Section V* のドリルの一部が収録されています．個人で学習する時にも，またクラスの授業でも効果的に利用できます．
吹込み者: Anne Bowers, Laura Bowers, Austin Hicks, Eric Kelso, Daniel Woods, Julia Yermakov

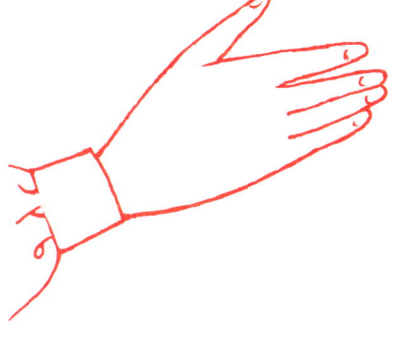

Lesson One

HOW DO YOU DO?
はじめまして

Section I PRESENTATION[1] CD1-1

In the States,[2] when we[3] see friends, we greet them with the phrase: "How are you?" Greetings are exchanged among friends, co-workers and even strangers[4]. But we do not often ask family members "How are you?" The lesson title "How do you do?" is a more formal greeting.

アメリカでは，友人と顔を合わせれば「お元気ですか」とあいさつを交わします．友人同士，職場の人たちや面識のない人でもあいさつを交わします．でも家族との間では「お元気ですか」とはしょっちゅう言いません．この課の題名「はじめまして，よろしく」はあらたまったあいさつの言い方です．

---

1) **Presentation** 解説．
2) **the States** 米国，アメリカ．
3) **we** この場合 the States を受けて米国人，アメリカ人の意味．
4) **strangers** 面識のない（初対面の）人々．

Section II APPLICATION DIALOGUES[1] CD1-2

Listen and repeat

Greetings—I

A Good morning. How are you today?
B Fine, thanks. How are you?
A Fine. How's your mother?
B She's fine, too. Thanks.
A That's good. Please give her my regards.[2]
B Thank you. I will.
A Well, I'll be seeing you. So long.
B So long.

（あいさつ—1）

おはようございます。お元気ですか。
ええ、おかげさまで。あなたは？
元気です。お母さんはどうしていらっしゃいますか。
ええ、元気ですよ。
それはよかった。どうぞお母さんによろしく。
ありがとう。伝えます。
ではまたね。さようなら。
さようなら。

Greetings—II

A Hello. How are you today?
B I'm fine, thanks. And you?
A Well, I have a cold.
B That's too bad. I hope you get well soon.
A Thank you. I'm sure I will.

（あいさつ—2）

やあ！お元気ですか。
ありがとう。元気です。あなたは？
それが、風邪でね。
それはいけませんね。早くよくなってください。
ありがとう。すぐよくなると思います。

Introductions

George Hello, Mary. How are you?

（紹介）

ジョージ: やあ、メアリー元気かい？

---

1) **Application Dialogues** 応用対話．
2) **give her my regards** 彼女にどうぞよろしく．

Lessone One

Mary　Fine, thanks. And you?
George　Fine. Let me introduce my friend. Mary Smith, John Jones.
John　How do you do,[1] Ms Smith? I'm glad to meet you.[2]
Mary　How do you do, Mr. Jones? I'm glad to meet you, too.

メアリー：ええ，元気よ．あなたは？
ジョージ：ぼくも元気だよ．友達を紹介しよう．メアリー・スミスさん，こちらジョン・ジョーンズさんです．
ジョン：こんにちは，スミスさんですか．はじめまして．
メアリー：こんにちは．ジョーンズさん．はじめてお目にかかります．

▥Thanks　（感謝／お礼）

A　I had a very good time[3] at your party. Thanks a lot.
B　You're welcome. Please come again soon.
A　Thank you. I will.[4] Goodbye.
B　Goodbye.

お宅のパーティは，とても楽しかったですよ．どうもありがとう．
どういたしまして．また近いうちにおいでください．
ありがとう．そうさせていただきます．さようなら．
さようなら．

▥Requests―I　（依頼／人に～を頼む）

A　May I use your car this afternoon?
B　Sure. Go right ahead.[5] Here are the

今日の午後あなたの車を使わせていただけますか．
ええ．どうぞどうぞ．はい鍵

---

1) **How do you do～?** は初対面のときに用いる言い方で，「はじめまして，よろしく」という意味．
2) 先に言ったほうは
   I'm glad to meet you.
   あとから言ったほうは
   I'm glad to meet you, too.
3) **have a（very）good time** 楽しいひとときを過ごす．
4) **I will.** ＜ I will come again soon. 実際上，I will は忠告・指図・依頼等に対する肯定の返事で，「そうします」「承知しました」などの意味に相当する．
5) **Go right ahead.** どうぞ（お使いください）．

keys.[1] です.
A　Thanks. どうもありがとう.
B　Don't mention it. But be careful. どういたしまして. でも気を
　 つけてくださいよ.
A　I will. Don't worry. 気をつけます. ご心配なく.

Requests—II　（依頼／人に〜を頼む）—2

A　May I have your card? 名刺をいただけませんか.
B　Sure. Here you are.[2] いいですよ. はいどうぞ.
A　Thank you very much. どうもありがとう.
B　You're welcome. どういたしまして.

Section III　NOTES ON CONVERSATIONAL STYLE[3]

1. Greetings（あいさつ）　Good morning. を使うのは，ふつう正午まで，または昼食を食べるまでです. Good afternoon. と Good evening. は，どちらかというと，あらたまった言い方で，日常その代りに使う言い方は，Hello. や Hi. です. Good night. を使うのは，夜，別れのあいさつをするときだけで，「おやすみなさい」と同じです. 人に会ったときに，あいさつとして使うことはけっしてありません.

　Goodbye. はふつうに使う別れのあいさつです. So long. は，くだけた言い方です. 仲よしの友達だけに使います. I'll be seeing you. も，非公式のもので，くだけた言い方です. 目上の人には，使ってはいけません. See you again. や Bye bye. もくだけた言い方なので，使いようによっては失礼になりかねません. 自信ができるまで初心者は避けたほうがよいでしょう.

　How are you? と言われて，Thank you. だけでやめてしまうのはいけません. Fine. とか，Very well. とか，Not so well. とかを添えて答えます. それ

---

1) **Here are the keys.** 鍵を手渡しながら言う.
2) **Here you are.** 相手の求めているものを手渡すときに使う表現.
3) **Notes on Conversational Style** 会話には，会話独特の言い回しやスタイルがあって，それについての注意.

から相手の機嫌（きげん）を尋ねるのです．それをしないと失礼にあたります．

  Correct: —How are you today?
      —Fine, thank you. How are you?
      —Not so well.
      —Oh, that's too bad.
  Strange: —How are you today?
      —Thank you.
      —Oh, oh, it's a nice day today, isn't it?

2. Introductions（紹介）　人を紹介する一番簡単な言い方は:
 Mr. A, (this is) Mr. B. (A さん，こちらは B さんです)
のように，年上の人か目上の人の名前を先に言います．上の例でいうと Mr. A のほうが Mr. B より年上，または目上です．また，男性と女性の場合は，まず女性に男性を紹介します．上の例で Mr. A のところが Ms. A または Mrs. A になるわけです．簡単な言い方であるかぎり，この方式はいつも正しく，またごく一般に使われる言い方です．なお主語は必ず this で，that, he, she では紹介になりません．

3. Thanks（感謝）　あらたまった言い方としては，Thank you very much. ですが，もっと会話的な言い方は，Thanks a lot. か Thanks. です．目上の人に言う場合には，もちろんあらたまった言い方を使うべきです．それに答えるには，次のような言い方があります．

 a. —Thank you very much for this lovely present.
   —*You're welcome.*（どういたしまして）
 b. —I must be leaving now. Thank you for a very pleasant evening.
   —*Don't mention it.* Come again soon.（とんでもありません．またどうぞいらしてください）

c. —This is a great present, John. Thanks a lot.
      —*Not at all.*〈くだけた言い方〉I'm glad you like it.
   d. —Thanks for helping me with my homework.
      —Sure. *Any time.*〈ごくくだけた言い方〉

▍**4. Requests**（依頼）　人に～を頼む場合の一番簡単な言い方は May I …? / Can I …? です．別の言い方として Do [Would] you mind if I …? があります．May I / Can I で始まる場合の答としては，Yes, you may. / Yes, you can. または Go right ahead. か No, you may not. / No, you cannot. または I wish you wouldn't.〈友達どうしなどで〉を使います．Do you mind で始まる場合の答には Not at all. を使います．断る場合には，まず I'm sorry, but… と言います．

   a. —May I use your dictionary this afternoon?
      —Yes, go right ahead. / I'm sorry, but I have to use it myself.
   b. —Do you mind if I smoke?
      —Not at all. Go right ahead. / I'm sorry, but I have a bad cold. I wish you wouldn't.

Section IV PRONUNCIATION DRILL[1]　CD1-3

　英語を上手に発音したいと思えば，次の3つのことがらを学ばなければなりません．すなわち，正しい sounds（音），正しい stress（強勢），正しい intonation（抑揚）です．この課では英語の発音のあらましを述べることにします．

▍**1. 英語の音**　ごく普通に vowels（母音）と consonants（子音）に大別されます．母音は，口腔内の摩擦が少なく，肺から出る呼気がなんらかの摩擦を起こして出される音のことです．したがって，母音は，口腔形状・舌の位置・

---

1) **Pronunciation Drill**　発音練習.

筋肉の緊張度などによって決定されます．まず，英語の 11 の母音について，つぎの口腔図を参照しながら音声を聞いて発音してみましょう．

Listen and repeat

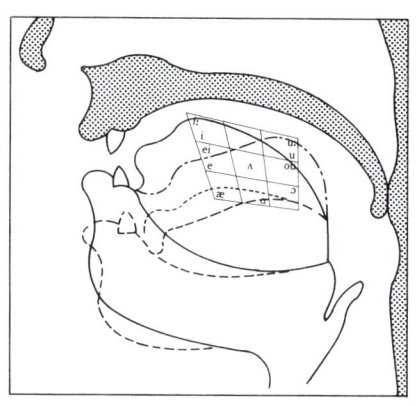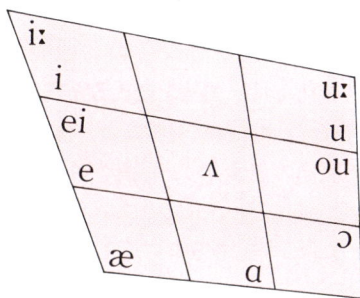

▓ 2. Pronunciation of [iː] and [i]（[iː] と [i] の発音）　[iː] の発音は，日本語の[イー]とほとんど同じです．にっこりと微笑したときのように，唇の左右が横に引かれます．写真をとるとき，カメラを持った人が，写される人に向かって，よく Say cheese.（はい，チーズ）と言いますが，それは，cheese には，[iː] の音が含まれているからです．[iː] は，微笑した顔で[イー]と言ったときの音，と覚えておきましょう．

　[i] の発音は，[iː] とは違います．[i] は，日本語の[イ]と[エ]の中間の音です．[i] をよく聞くと，[イ]ともつかず，[エ]ともつかない音です．[i] は [iː] の短い形ではありません．全く別の音です．

　[iː] と [i] の区別を，練習して覚えましょう．

Listen and repeat

1. heat [hiːt]　　　hit [hit]
2. heed [hiːd]　　　hid [hid]
3. seat [siːt]　　　sit [sit]

4. meat [miːt]　　　mitt [mit]
5. sheep [ʃiːp]　　　ship [ʃip]

3. Stress（強勢）
強勢とは，強く言うか弱く言うかということです．日本語では，特に語調を強めて言うようなとき以外は，強く言うか弱く言うかは，ほとんど問題になりません．たとえば，「雨」と言うとき，áme のように a を強くしても，amé と me を強くしても，意味は変わりません．しかし，声の高さを変えると，a̲me（雨），ame̲（飴）のように別の語になります．

英語では，強勢を変えると別の語になることがあります．たとえば，désert（砂漠），desért（見捨てる）のようになります．

英語の発音では，強勢が非常に大切です．強いところと弱いところが，きれいに組み合わされてリズム（rhythm）を作ります．リズミカルな英語を話すためには，常に強勢に注意しなければなりません．

Listen and repeat
1. the teácher [də dá də]
2. the cómpany [də dá də də]
3. the Énglish class [də dá də də]
4. Hów do you dó? [dá də də dá]
5. It's níce to sée you. [də dá də dá də]
6. Gíve me a piece of bréad. [dá də də də də dá]

4. Intonation（抑揚）
話すときの声の高さの上げ下げのことを pitch（音程）と言いますが，抑揚とは，音程の変化によって生じる音調のことです．先に述べた強勢がリズムを作るのに対して，抑揚は，いわばメロディーを形成します．日本語では，音程は語単位で現われますが，英語では，音程による抑揚は文になってはじめて現われます．英語では，語単位で現われるのは強勢であることを思い出してください．

次の日本語を，普通に発音してごらんなさい．ローマ字で書き換えた部分の線は，音程の変化（日本語ではこれをアクセントと言います）を表わします．

Lesson One

たとえば，ashi の音程を変えて ashi と言うと，「足」が「(植物の)あし」になってしまいます．haru「春」と haru「張る」の関係も同じです．

これに対して英語では，音程は，文に現われて抑揚となるときが問題なので，たとえば English という単語を，English と発音しても，音程を変えて English と発音しても，語の意味に変りはありません．英語の語で重要なのは，前節に述べた強勢です．

日本人学習者の発音を聞いていますと，音程と強勢を混同している場合が多いように思われます．あるいは，強勢を音程ですり替えていると言ってもよいでしょう．次の 2 つの文を聞いてごらんなさい．はじめの文は不自然な抑揚で，2 番目の文が自然な抑揚の発音です．

Listen and repeat

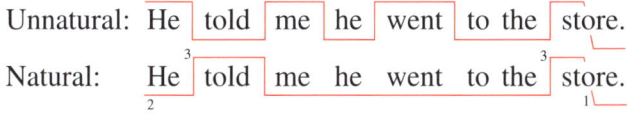

英語では音程の変化は 4 種類に区別されるのが普通です．すなわち，1 (低い)，2 (並)，3 (高い)，4 (ごく高い) の 4 つです．抑揚を表わす線を intonation curve (抑揚曲線) と言いますが，抑揚曲線と数字の関係は次の通りです．

語または音節 syllable のすぐ上の線は 3 を示します．4 の線は 3 より少し高い線で示しますが，実際には，驚き・強調その他を表わす特別の場合以外には現われません．

You want to go there!

(あなたがそこへ行きたいって！とんでもない)

また，垂直の線は音節 syllable の音での音程の変化を示し，斜線は音節内での音程の変化を示します．

Section V PATTERN USAGE DRILL[1] CD1-4

Directions: Practice the following exercises until you can do them smoothly with natural pronunciation. If you have difficulty understanding the point of an exercise, refer again to the explanation in Section III. In doing exercises requiring two speakers, you may take both parts yourself or practice with a friend.

> 手びき：正しいリズムと抑揚，それにできるだけ英語らしい発音で言えるまで，次の練習問題をしましょう．練習問題の内容についてわからない点があったら，Section III の説明を見てください．2人の話者を必要とする練習では，1人2役でやるか，または友達と2人でしましょう．

Listen and repeat
指示に従って練習しなさい．

1. 学習者が自己紹介をする．
　例) Let me introduce myself. My name is Sumiko Fujisawa.
　　　Let me introduce myself. My name is Akio Nishi.

2. 2人の学習者がおたがいに紹介し合う．
　例) Let me introduce myself. My name is Sumiko Fujisawa. /

---

1) **Pattern Usage Drill** 文型運用練習．

How do you do? My name is Akio Nishi. / How do you do?

3. 先生が１人の学習者を他の学習者に紹介する．
例）Let me introduce you. Ms. Fujisawa, Mr. Nishi. /
How do you do, Mr. Nishi? I'm glad to meet you. /
How do you do, Ms. Fujisawa? I'm glad to meet you, too.

4. 学習者がクラスメートの１人を他のクラスメートに紹介する．
例）Let me introduce you. Ms. Fujisawa, Mr. Nishi. /
How do you do, Mr. Nishi? I'm glad to meet you. /
How do you do, Ms. Fujisawa? I'm glad to meet you, too.

5. １人の学習者が先生を別の学習者に紹介する．
例）Let me introduce my teacher. Mr. Crane, Ms. Fujisawa. /
How do you do, Ms. Fujisawa? I'm glad to meet you. /
How do you do, Mr. Crane? I'm glad to meet you, too.

6. 学習者がクラスメートの１人を他のクラスメートに紹介する．
例）Let me introduce my classmate. Ms. Oda, Ms. Suzuki. /
How do you do? I'm glad to meet you. / How do you do? I'm glad to meet you, too.

7. 先生がクラスのめいめいに次のようにあいさつする．
例）Good afternoon.［Good morning. / Good evening.］How are you today? / Fine, thanks. And you? / Fine, thanks.

8. 学習者がクラスのめいめいに次のようにあいさつする．
例）Hello, Ms. Fujisawa. / Hello, Mr. Nishi.

9. 学習者がおたがいに次のようにあいさつする．

例）Hello, Ms. Fujisawa. How are you today? / Fine, thanks. How are you, Mr. Nishi? / Fine, thanks.

10. 先生が学習者に次の人々の様子を聞く．

例）How's your mother? / She's fine, thanks. / That's good. Please give her my regards. / Thank you. I will.

（次の語句を使って言い換えなさい）

1. your father
2. your brother
3. your sister
4. your grandmother
5. your grandfather
6. your uncle
7. your mother
8. Mr. Fujimoto
9. Mr. Baker
10. Mrs. Stone

11. 問題10を今度は学習者どうしでやる．

12. 学習者どうしが相手の様子を聞く．

例）How are you today? / Well, I have a cold. / That's too bad. I hope you get well soon. / Thanks. I'm sure I will.

（次の語句を使って言い換えなさい）

1. a headache 頭痛
2. a toothache 歯痛
3. an upset stomach 胃痛
4. an earache 耳の痛み
5. a bad cold 悪性の風邪
6. a slight headache 軽い頭痛
7. a sore throat 喉の痛み
8. the flu 流行性感冒（インフルエンザ）
9. a backache 背中の痛み
10. a stiff shoulder 肩凝り

13. 例にならい，学習者はおたがいに何か物を与え，おたがいに礼を言う（次の語句を使って言い換え，物を渡すときには 'Here's ＿＿＿．' と言うこと）．

例) Here's a book. / Thanks a lot. / You're welcome.

1. a pencil
2. a pen
3. a dictionary
4. a notebook
5. a watch
6. a handkerchief
7. a textbook
8. an English dictionary
9. a Japanese dictionary
10. a good book

14. 例にならい，次の語句を使って言い換えなさい．

例) May [Can] I use your pen? / Sure. Go right ahead. Here it is. / Thanks a lot. / You're welcome.

1. your pencil
2. your red pencil
3. your dictionary
4. your desk
5. your Japanese dictionary
6. your English dictionary
7. your eraser
8. your knife
9. your pen
10. your cell phone

15. 例にならい，次の語句を使って言い換えなさい．

例) May [Can] I have an apple? / Sure. Here you are. / Thanks a lot. / You're welcome.

1. a hundred yen
2. ten yen
3. a pencil
4. an orange
5. an eraser
6. a notebook
7. a thousand yen
8. your name card
9. your address
10. your phone number

16. 下線の部分に適切な語句を入れなさい．

A: Good morning. How ___ you today?
B: ___ fine, thanks.

A: Hello, Jack. How is _____ family?
B: They're fine, thanks. And _____?

A: How do you do? My name is Kim. It's so _____ to meet you.
B: Nice to meet you, _____. I'm Bill.

A: May I _____ your dictionary?
B: Sure. Go _____ ahead.

Lesson Two

MAY I ASK A QUESTION?
お尋ねしてもよろしいですか

Section I PRESENTATION CD1-5

In English, questions are used to get information and to keep the flow of a conversation. Not all questions are good. In Japan, personal questions are common, but in the States personal questions are taboo.

英語では(人に)何か尋ねるのはいろいろなことを知ったり，人との話がうまく進むようにするためです．しかし，なんでもかんでも尋ねてよいわけではありません．日本では個人的な話題が普通ですが，アメリカでは個人に関することは(絶対に)避けるべきことです．

Section II APPLICATION DIALOGUE CD1-6

Listen and repeat

A Hello. How are you today?　　やあ！どうですか，今日は．

B	Fine, thanks. And you?	おかげで，元気です．あなたは？
A	Fine, but I'm a little tired.	元気は元気ですが，ちょっと疲れています．
B	Oh? Did you swim this morning?	あら？けさ泳いだのですか．
A	Yes, I did. We[1] had a good time.	ええ，泳ぎました．楽しかったですよ．
B	Who went with you?	だれがいっしょだったのですか．
A	John did.	ジョン君です．
B	Does he like to swim?	彼は泳ぐのが好きですか．
A	Yes. He likes to swim very much. Do you like to swim?	ええ，彼は泳ぐのが大好きです．あなたは泳ぐのが好きですか．
B	No, I don't. I like to play tennis. I want to play this afternoon. Do you want to play, too?	いや，好きではありません．私はテニスをするのが好きです．今日の午後，やりたいと思っています．あなたもやりませんか．
A	Yes, I'd like to, but I have to work this afternoon.	したいのはやまやまですが，今日の午後は仕事がありますので．
B	Don't you go to school in the afternoon?	午後は学校へ行かないのですか．
A	No, I don't. I work at my father's store.	ええ，行っていません．父の店で働いています．
B	Do you have to work very hard?	そうとう身を入れて働かなくてはならないのですか．
A	Of course, I do. Don't you work at the library?	もちろんですよ．あなたは図書館で働いていないのですか．
B	No. I don't work at all. I just play tennis every day.	ええ，ぜんぜん働いていません．ただ毎日テニスをやるだけです．
A	I guess some people have all the	うまくやっている連中もいる

---

1) 相手が「私たち (We)」と言ったので，
 1人で行ったのではないことがわかる．

luck.[1]

B　See you.

なんて，うらやましいね.

後ほどお会いしましょう.

Section III　NOTES ON CONVERSATIONAL STYLE

1. 動詞の現在形（I play. We sing. など）　every day [morning, week など] や in the morning [evening, summer, fall など] は，動詞の現在形とともによく使います. he, she, it, その他第三者で単数を表わす語といっしょに使うとき，動詞の原形に s または es をつけ加えます.

 a. I play tennis every day. → John *plays* tennis every day.
 b. We go to the countryside every summer. → She *goes* to the countryside every summer.
 c. They study in the morning. → He *studies* in the afternoon.
 d. I work at my father's store. → He *works* at the library.
 e. I like tennis. → Mary *likes* tennis.

2. 動詞の過去形（I played. We sang. など）　規則動詞の過去形を作る規則は，Section IV に説明してあります. しばしば yesterday, last week [month, year] あるいは this morning [afternoon, evening] などのはっきりと過去の時を表わす副詞語句を伴います.

 a. I *worked* at my father's store last year.
 b. We *played* tennis this morning.
 c. He *swam* yesterday.
 d. They *studied* this afternoon.

---

1) **some people have all the luck**（＝are lucky）「まったくうまくやっている（うらやましいね）」.

3. Do [Does] をつけて作る疑問文

be 動詞以外の動詞を含む現在形の叙述文を疑問文にする場合，疑問を表わす符号ともいえる助動詞 do，もしくは does をつけ加えます。疑問であることを示すこれらの符号は，日本語の疑問を表わす符号ともいえる終助詞「か」とよく似ています。英語の符号は文のはじめに置きますが，日本語では文末に置きます。

> You play tennis every day. （あなたは毎日テニスをします）
> *Do* you play tennis every day? （あなたは毎日テニスをしますか）
> Yes, I do. （はい，します）
> No, I don't. （いいえ，しません）

このように助動詞を加えて作る疑問文では，He *studies*. や She *plays* tennis. などの動詞についている s は do に移って does となります。たとえば，

> He studies every day.
> Does he study every day?

be 動詞以外の動詞を含む過去形の叙述文を疑問文にする場合，過去の疑問を表わす符号 did を加えます。過去の動作であることは did だけでわかりますから，動詞自身は原形のままでよいのです。

> You played tennis yesterday.
> *Did* you play tennis yesterday? — Yes, I did. [No, I didn't.]
> *Did* he study last week? — Yes, he did. [No, he didn't.]

注意： もともと英語では主語と動詞を入れ替えることで疑問文を作っていました。今日でも be 動詞は昔ながらの習慣を守っていますが，一般動詞は代理の Do, Does を文頭に置くことで疑問文の特徴である「動詞＋主語」の語順をかろうじて維持しています。

▮▮▮▮ **4.** 次の文では，who, how, which などの疑問詞（あるいは疑問詞＋名詞）を文の主語と置き換えて作ってあります．このときは do, does, did は使いません．

    a. John swims every day.
    b. *Who* swims every day?
    c. *How many boys* swam yesterday?
    d. *Which dog* ran away?

▮▮▮▮ **5. 否定文**　be 動詞以外の一般動詞の現在形または過去形の文を否定文にする場合，次のように do not (= don't), does not (= doesn't), did not (= didn't) を使います．

    a. I like tennis. → I *don't* like tennis.
    b. John plays baseball every week. → John *doesn't* play baseball every week.
    c. We played tennis yesterday. → We *didn't* play tennis yesterday.

  注意：　もともと英語では動詞の後に not をおいて I know not … と言っていました．現代英語でも基本型は同じです．代理の動詞「Do, Does, Did」を本動詞に見立て「代理の動詞」＋ not の型を用いています．

▮▮▮▮ **6. 否定疑問文**　（negative questions）は話者の否定の態度を表わします．否定疑問に答える際の yes と no の使い方に注意してください．同じ質問に答えるにしても，日本語の用法と逆になることがあります．英語の yes/no は次に続く文の内容を先取りする働きがあります．

    a. Do you like tennis?（あなたはテニスが好きですか）
       ［好きかどうか聞いている］

Yes, I do.（はい，好きです）
No, I don't.（いいえ，好きではありません）
b. Don't you like tennis?（テニスが好きじゃないですか）
［聞く人は，相手がテニス好きではないと思っている］
Yes, I do.（いいえ，好きです）
No, I don't.（はい，好きではありません）

7. want, like や have などの一般動詞をほかの動詞とともに用いる場合は，あとが 'to ＋ 動詞の原形' の型になります．

a. I want *to play* tennis today.（私は今日テニスをしたい）
John wants *to swim* this afternoon.
（今日の午後ジョンは泳ぎたがっている）
We wanted *to work* at the bookstore last year.
（昨年私たちは書店で働きたかった）
She doesn't want *to study*.（彼女は勉強したがらない）
b. I like *to play* tennis.（私はテニスをするのが好きだ）
He likes *to swim*.（彼は泳ぐのが好きだ）
We liked *to work* at the bookstore.
（私たちは書店で働くのが好きだった）
c. I have *to study* every day.（私は毎日勉強をしなければならない）
She has *to study* every day.（彼女は毎日勉強をしなければならない）
We had *to work* yesterday.
（私たちは昨日出勤しなければならなかった）
I don't have to work.（私は働く必要がない）

Lesson Two

Section IV PRONUNCIATION DRILL CD1-7

1. Pronunciation of [ei] and [e] ([ei] と [e] の発音) [ei] は日本語の[エイ]とほとんど同じです．[e] は日本語の[エ]に近い音です．

Listen and repeat

1. bait [beit]   bet [bet]
2. mate [meit]   met [met]
3. date [deit]   debt [det]
4. gate [geit]   get [get]
5. pate [peit]   pet [pet]

2. Pronunciation of [ʌ] and [æ] ([ʌ] と [æ] の発音) ぼんやりしているとき，急に背中をたたかれると，「アッ」という声が出ることがあります．[ʌ] は，この声とほとんど同じです．あごは閉じていませんが，といって，それほど開き過ぎもせず，中くらいです．

[æ] は [ʌ] よりは，あごを開きます．ここで「あ」と言うと日本語の[ア]です．日本語の[ア]を言うときは，舌の奥のほうは，上の奥歯に触れていません．[æ] のときは，舌の奥のほうを上の奥歯に触れるようにします(p.7 参照)．もともと æ という記号は a と e を組み合せて作った文字です．[エ]という構えのまま[ア]と言うと，[æ] になることがあります．ためしてみてください．

Listen and repeat

1. but [bʌt]   bat [bæt]
2. hut [hʌt]   hat [hæt]
3. mud [mʌd]   mad [mæd]
4. cut [kʌt]   cat [kæt]
5. cup [kʌp]   cap [kæp]

Exercise: 例にならって上の各組の語を用いて問答をしなさい．

例) Did you say *but*? — No. I said *bat*.

3. 2–3–1 抑揚パターン　叙述文や who, what, which, where そのほか同じような疑問詞で始まる疑問文は 2–3–1 抑揚パターンで，これが基本です。しかし do, does, did などで始まる疑問文には使わないのが普通です。

Listen and repeat

1. I like to play tennis.
2. Who works at the bookstore?
3. I have to work this afternoon.

規則：2 で始め，最後の重要な語の，強い強勢のある音節を 3 で言い，その後は 1 で言います。

Listen and repeat

1. Who [Whom] did you see yesterday?

    I saw your mother yesterday.

2. When did you see my mother?

    I saw her yesterday.

Exercise: カッコ内に指示してある疑問に答える形で，次の各文を発音してごらんなさい。

例) John likes milk. (what) John likes milk.

   (who) John likes milk.

1. Bill hit the ball in the park. (where, what, who)
2. John took his sister to the movie. (where, who, whom)
3. Mary played tennis yesterday. (who, what, when)
4. I went to the countryside last week. (where, when, which week, who)

5. Susie gave me some candy. (who, whom, what)

4. Yes か No で答えられる疑問文には **2–3** の抑揚を使います．

Listen and repeat

—Who swam yesterday?
—I did.
—Did you play tennis?
—No. I don't like tennis.
—Do you like baseball?
—Yes. I do.

規則：2 で始めて，最後の重要な語の，強い強勢のある音節を 3 で言い，そのまま終わりまで 3 で行きます．ただし文末で声をもう少しあげてもかまいません．

5. Pronunciation of regular verb past forms （規則動詞の過去形の発音）

Listen and repeat

(1) [d] 以外の有声音で終わる規則動詞は [d] を加えるだけで過去形となります．

　　play [plei]　　　　played [pleid]
　　study [stʌ́di]　　　studied [stʌ́did]
　　rub [rʌb]　　　　 rubbed [rʌbd]

(2) [t] 以外の無声音で終わる規則動詞は [t] を加えるだけで過去形となります．

　　work [wɚk]　　　　worked [wɚkt]

stop [stɑp]	stopped [stɑpt]
wash [wɑʃ]	washed [wɑʃt]

(3) [t] または [d] で終わる規則動詞は [id] を加えれば過去形となります。

want [wɑnt]	wanted [wɑ́ntid]
end [end]	ended [éndid]

6. Pronunciation of irregular verb past forms （不規則動詞の過去形の発音）　不規則動詞の場合，過去形はいろいろな形をとりますが，本課では次の動詞をとりあげました。

Listen and repeat

have [hæv]	had [hæd]
swim [swim]	swam [swæm]
go [gou]	went [went]

Section V PATTERN USAGE DRILL CD1-8

Directions to the instructor: The following exercises are designed to give the students fluency in the patterns introduced in Section II. Drills utilizing the charts at the back of the book are meant to introduce the patterns. Such drills are followed by exercises of other kinds: substitution, conversion, conversation, and others. Each exercise should be considered a drill in pronunciation as well as in structure. Make careful correction of the student's pronunciation from the very beginning. Do not go on to a new exercise until the student exhibits satisfactory command of the exercise at hand. The problems drilled in Section V of this and the following lessons are completely explained in Section III of each lesson. Section III should be assigned for study at home, thus saving valuable classroom time for drills. In the classroom the instructor's role is to provide a living model of the stream of English speech for the students to imitate. In each exercise the instructor should pronounce each item and the student should repeat. After the exercise has been drilled using mim-mem, the students should do it again themselves. Remember: the exercises are not tests; the instructor is not a tester. He is a source of English for the student to imitate; the following exercises are source material for the instructor.

> 手びき: 各課の Section V の練習問題は，本書の巻末にある Chart を応用したものです．正しい抑揚，それからできるだけ英語らしい発音で言えるまで，それぞれの練習をしましょう．これらの問題は Section III に説明のある各項目の豊富な練習教材になるでしょう．練習問題についてわからない点があったら，Section III の説明を見てください．

Listen and repeat

1. ⇒ Chart I. まず巻末の Chart I を開いてよく絵を見ます．それから学習者は本を閉じて，今度は先生のあとについて，それぞれの絵にある動作を英語で言いなさい．学習者がチャートの内容に完全に慣れるまでこの練習をくり返すこと．

1. I play baseball every day.
2. I work at the bookstore every day.
3. I teach every day.
4. I go to the movies every day.
5. I swim every day.
6. I work in the garden every day.
7. I go to the store every day.

8. I play tennis every day.
9. I skate every day.

2. ⇒ Chart I. (Chart I を使って言い換えなさい。以下同じ)
1. Instructor: Bob
   Student: He plays baseball every day.
2. Sally
3. Professor McCarthy
4. William
5. Eddie
6. Charles
7. Sachiko
8. Mr. Forster
9. Mr. Johnson

3. ⇒ Chart I.
1. We / We play baseball every day.
2. He
3. Professor McCarthy
4. William
5. You
6. They
7. Sachiko
8. I
9. She

4. ⇒ Chart I.
1. Bob / Bob plays baseball every day.
   Bob and Dick / Bob and Dick play baseball every day.
   I / I play baseball every day.
   You / You play baseball every day.
   He / He plays baseball every day.
2. Sally / Sally and Harry / I / you / we
3. Professor McCarthy / I / he / you / she
4. William / you / they / we / she
5. Eddie / he / they / you / she

6. Charles / we / she / you / he
7. Sachiko / we / they / he / you
8. Mr. Forster / he / we / she / they
9. Mr. Johnson / he / she / you / they

5. 例にならい，次の各文の主語を換えて言いなさい．
   例) You swim every summer. / He / He swims every summer.
   1. You go to school every day. / She
   2. You like Sally. / He
   3. You skate every winter. / Bob
   4. You play golf every Saturday. / Mr. Crane
   5. You work every day. / My father
   6. You sing every morning. / She
   7. You go to church every Sunday. / My brother
   8. You play *shogi* every Saturday. / My brother
   9. You like tennis. / My sister
   10. You go to the library every afternoon. / My teacher

6. ⇒ Chart I.
   1. Do you play baseball every day? / No, I don't. Bob plays baseball every day.

   (以下続ける)

7. 例にならい，問題 5 の各文を疑問文にして，肯定で答えなさい．
   例) You swim every summer. / Do you swim every summer? / Yes, I do. I swim every summer.

8. 例にならい，問題 5 の各文を疑問文にして，否定で答えなさい．

例）You swim every summer. / Do you swim every summer? / No, I don't. I don't swim every summer.

9. 例にならい，問題 5 の各文を he を使って疑問文にして，肯定で答えなさい．

例）You swim every summer. / Does he swim every summer? / Yes. He swims every summer.

10. 例にならい，問題 5 の各文を she を使って疑問文にして，否定で答えなさい．

例）You swim every summer. / Does she swim every summer? / No. She doesn't swim every summer.

11. ⇒ Chart I.
1. You play baseball every Sunday. / No. I don't play baseball every Sunday. I play baseball every Monday.

（以下続ける）

12. ⇒ Chart I.
1. Does Dick play baseball every Sunday? / Yes, he does. Do you play baseball every Sunday? / No, I don't. I don't play baseball.

（以下続ける）

13. 例にならい，問題 5 の各文をまず you を主語とする疑問文に，次に Bill を主語とする疑問文にして，それぞれ否定で答えなさい．

例）You swim every summer. / Do you swim every summer? / No. I don't swim every summer. Does Bill swim every summer? / No. He doesn't swim every summer.

Lesson Two

14. ⇒ Chart I.
1. (in the morning) Dick plays baseball in the morning. Do you play baseball in the morning? / Yes. I play baseball in the morning.
    (in the afternoon) Dick plays baseball in the afternoon. Do you play baseball in the afternoon? / Yes. I play baseball in the afternoon.
2. every Monday / in the afternoon
3. in the morning / every Tuesday
4. in the evening / every Wednesday
5. in the afternoon / every Thursday
6. in the morning / every spring
7. every day / in the afternoon
8. every summer / every afternoon
9. every winter / in the winter

15. 例にならい，対話を完成しなさい。ただし，質問には in the morning [afternoon, evening, winter, summer, fall, spring], every day [morning, afternoon, evening, winter, summer, fall, spring] を使うこと。

例) Do you go to the movies every day? / No. I don't go to the movies every day. I go every Saturday.
Do you play *shogi* in the morning? / No. I don't play *shogi* in the morning. I play in the evening.

1. work in the yard
2. go to the beach
3. go to the mountains
4. play golf
5. study English
6. study history
7. go to the bookstore
8. skate
9. swim
10. go to the park

16. ⇒ Chart I.
  1. They played baseball yesterday.
  2. He worked at the bookstore yesterday.
  3. taught   6. worked   9. skated
  4. went   7. went
  5. swam   8. played

17. 例にならい，次の各文を言い換えなさい．
  例) I study music every day. / I studied music yesterday. / He studied music yesterday.
  1. I have a headache today. (had)
  2. I meet Professor McCarthy every day. (met)
  3. I teach every day. (taught)
  4. I use my dictionary every day.
  5. I ask a question in every class. (the last class)
  6. I practice English sentences every day.
  7. I swim every day. (swam)
  8. I work every day.
  9. I play golf every day.
  10. I study English every day.

18. ⇒ Chart I.
  1. They played baseball last Sunday.
  2. He worked at the bookstore last Monday.
  3. He taught English last Tuesday.
  (以下続ける)

19. 例にならい，問題 17 の各文に last week, last month, last Saturday など

の語句を加えて過去の文に言い換えなさい.

例) I study music every day. / Oh?[1] I studied music last Saturday.

20. ⇒ Chart I.
1. Did Bob play baseball yesterday? / Yes, he did.

(以下続ける)

21. 例にならい，問題 17 の各文を過去の疑問文にして，否定で答えなさい.

例) I study music every day. / Did you study music yesterday? / No, I didn't.

22. 例にならい，問題 17 の各文を言い換えなさい.

例) I study music every day. / Oh? I don't study music every day. I didn't study yesterday.

23. ⇒ Chart I.
1. I like to play baseball.

(以下続ける)

24. ⇒ Chart I.
1. Do you like to play baseball? / No, I don't. Dick likes to play baseball.

(以下続ける)

25. ⇒ Chart I.
1. I like to play baseball. / Oh? Don't you like to work at the bookstore? / No, I don't. Harry likes to work at the bookstore.

---

1) **Oh?** ああそうですか.

2. I like to work at the bookstore. / Oh? Don't you like to teach? / No, I don't. Professor McCarthy likes to teach.
（以下続ける）

26. 例にならい，問題 15 の語句を使って否定疑問文を作り，肯定で答えなさい．

例）(go to the movies) → Don't you like to go to the movies? / Yes, I do. I like to go to the movies very much.

27. ⇒ Chart I.
1. Do you want to play baseball? / No. I don't want to play baseball. I want to work at the bookstore.
2. Do you want to work at the bookstore? / No. I don't want to work at the bookstore. I want to teach.

（以下続ける）

28. ⇒ Chart I.
1. Does Bob want to play baseball today? / No. He doesn't want to play baseball. He wants to work at the bookstore.
2. Does Sally want to work at the bookstore today? / No. She doesn't want to work at the bookstore. She wants to go to school.

（以下続ける）

29. 例にならい，問題 15 の語句を用いて言いなさい．

例）(go to the movies) → I like to go to the movies. I want to go to the movies this afternoon.

30. 例にならい，問いと答を言いなさい．

例）Do you want to swim this afternoon? / No, thank you. I have to work this afternoon.

1. go to the movies / study English
2. go to the beach / work at my father's store
3. go to the mountains / study history
4. play tennis / visit a friend
5. skate / go to church
6. go to the park / stay home
7. play golf / work
8. play the piano / study German
9. go to the park / go to school
10. go to the library / visit my brother

31. ⇒ Chart I.

1. Doesn't Bob want to play baseball? / Yes, he does. But he has to work at the bookstore today.
2. Doesn't Harry want to work at the bookstore? / Yes, he does. But he has to go to school today.

（以下続ける）

32. 例にならい，次の語句を使って問いと答を言いなさい．

例）Do you have to go to school today? / No. I don't have to go to school today.

1. work this afternoon
2. work at the bookstore
3. work at the grocery store
4. work at your father's store
5. go home now
6. study German tonight
7. work at the store in the morning

8. study history now
9. teach English today
10. study in the evening

33. 例にならい，次の語句を使って問いと答を言いなさい．

例) Do you like to swim? / No, I don't. I like to ski. I want to ski this afternoon.

1. play golf
2. skate
3. play chess
4. play *shogi*
5. go to the library
6. go to the movies
7. go to the park
8. go to the lake
9. go to the mountains
10. study English

34. 例にならい，問題 33 の語句を使って過去の文を作り，それに問いかける文と答を言いなさい．

例) I swam this afternoon. / Oh? Who swam with you? / John did.

35. ⇒ Chart I.
1. How many boys played baseball? / I don't know.
2. How many boys worked at the bookstore? / I don't know.

（以下続ける）

36. ⇒ Chart I.
1. Who wants to play baseball now? / Bob does.
2. Who wants to work at the bookstore now? / Sally does.

（以下続ける）

37. ⇒ Chart I.
1. I played baseball yesterday. / Oh? Didn't you work at the bookstore? / No, I didn't.

2. I worked at the bookstore yesterday. / Oh? Didn't you go to school? / No, I didn't.
（以下続ける）

38. 例にならい，次の語を使って言い換えなさい．
例) I'm a little tired. (hungry) → I'm a little hungry. (thirsty) → I'm a little thirsty.

1. late
2. early
3. hungry
4. sad
5. sick
6. warm
7. cold
8. worried
9. surprised
10. disappointed
11. ill
12. angry

39. 次の話を読み，問いに答えなさい．

Bill is a little tired now. He swam this morning. His friend John went with him. They had a very good time. Bill and John like to swim very much. Bill's friend Harry doesn't like to swim. He likes to play tennis. He wants to play this afternoon. Harry doesn't work. He just plays tennis every day. He doesn't have to work.

1. How's Bill now?
2. Why?
3. Who went with him?
4. Did they have a good time?
5. Do they like to swim?
6. Does Harry like to swim?
7. Doesn't Harry want to swim this afternoon?
8. Does Bill want to play tennis this afternoon?
9. Does Harry work?
10. Why not?

40. 下線の部分に適切な語句を入れなさい.

A: Did you _____ to work today?
B: Yes, but I was a _____ late.

A: Do you like _____ play soccer?
B: Yes, I like to _____ very much.

A: Does _____ friend like to swim?
B: Yes, he _____ it very much.

A: Did you work _____ last night?
B: Yes, I _____ until 11:30.

Lesson Three
A SPOON AND SOME ICE CREAM
スプーンとアイスクリーム

Section I Presentation　CD1-9

In Japan, restaurants have "set menus," you choose Set A or Set B. But in the States, you must choose the type of potato, salad dressing, vegetable and how you want your meat cooked.[1] When we are offered food or drinks, we need to say what we want in a polite way.

日本ではレストランに行くと「セットA: セットB」などのセットメニューから料理を選ぶことになります。しかしアメリカではポテト, サラダのドレッシング, 野菜などの料理法や肉の焼き具合をはっきりさせなければなりません. 食べものや飲みものが出される場合, 自分の注文をていねいにはっきりさせることが必要です.

---

1) **how you want your meat cooked** （注文する）肉の焼き具合. rare（生焼け）, medium（中くらい）, well-done（よく焼いた）のように指定する.

Section II APPLICATION DIALOGUES CD1-10

Listen and repeat

A   What a delicious meal!

B   Thank you. Would you like some coffee now?

A   No, thank you. I prefer tea.[1)]

B   Do you use sugar in your tea?

A   No. I don't use sugar. How about you?

B   I use a little sugar and a little cream. Would you like some fruit?

A   Yes, thank you. Do you have any apples?

B   Yes. Try one of these apples. They're very sweet.

A   Thank you. Hmmm. These're delicious.

B   Fruit is very cheap now. Apples are only $1.00 a pound.[2)]

A   Is that so? I don't want to trouble you, but I'd like a glass of water.

B   Wouldn't you like some cold juice?

ごちそうさまでした！

どういたしまして．コーヒーになさいますか．

いいえ，結構です．紅茶のほうがいいのですが．

紅茶に砂糖をお入れになりますか．

いいえ，砂糖は入れません．あなたはどうですか．

私は砂糖を少しとクリームを少し入れます．果物はいかがですか．

ええ，ありがとうございます．リンゴはありますか．

ええ，このリンゴを1つ召しあがってごらんなさい．とても甘いですよ．

ありがとう．うん．これはおいしい．

いま果物はとても安いんですよ．リンゴだって1ポンドでわずか1ドルです．

そうですか．ご面倒ですが，水を1杯いただきたいですね．

冷たいジュースをお飲みになりませんか．

---

1) **prefer tea**（to coffee）= like tea better（than coffee）.   2) **pound**（重さの単位）約453グラム．

Lesson Three

A　No, thank you. I don't like juice. I prefer water.
B　Oh, how strange! I don't like water. I prefer juice.

いいえ，けっこうです．ジュースは好きではありませんので．水のほうがいいんです．
おや，妙ですね．私は水はいやですよ．ジュースのほうがいいですね．

A　I want to buy a shirt.
B　Would you like a dress shirt[1] or a sport shirt?
A　A dress shirt. I'd like a plain[2] white one.
B　This one is nice. It's inexpensive, too. It's only nineteen and a half dollars.
A　Fine. I want a tie, too.
B　We have some very nice ties here.
A　I like this blue one.
B　Yes. It's very nice. It's only eighteen dollars and twenty five cents.
A　Fine. I'll take them.
B　Certainly.

シャツを買いたいのですが．
ワイシャツですか，スポーツシャツですか．
ワイシャツです．無地の白いのがほしいのですが．
これはなかなかよい品です．値段も安いですよ．たった19ドル半でございます．
けっこう．ネクタイもほしいのですが．
こちらにとてもよいのがございます．
この青いのが気に入りました．
そうですね．これはとてもすてきでございますね．お値段もわずか18ドル25セントでございます．
はい，それをいただきます．
承知いたしました．

---

1) **dress shirt** shirt だけでもワイシャツのことだが，ここでは sport shirt と区別するため dress shirt「きちんとした正式のワイシャツ」と言っている．
2) **plain** [plein] 無地の．

Section III NOTES ON CONVERSATIONAL STYLE

1. Would you like 〜? は Do you want 〜? のよりていねいな言い方です．

 Do you want some coffee?（コーヒーを飲むかい）

 Would you like some coffee?（コーヒーを召しあがりますか）

人が頼んだ以外の物をすすめたい場合に用いる言い方は wouldn't を伴う否定疑問を使います．

 —I want some water.（私は水がほしいのですが）

 —*Wouldn't* you *like* some cold juice?

 （冷たいジュースはおいやですか）

would like はていねいな言い方の叙述文に用います．I would like は，ふつうの会話では [aid laik] と発音し，I'd like とつづることがあります．

 a. I want some coffee.（コーヒーがほしい）

  I'd like some coffee.（コーヒーをいただきたいのです）

 b. I want to play tennis.（テニスをやりたい）

  I'd like to play tennis.（テニスをやりたいものです）

 c. I want to meet him.（彼に会いたい）

  I'd like to meet him.（彼にお会いしたいのです）

2. 数えられる名詞；数えられない名詞；単数；複数

日本語の名詞は単数・複数の区別をしませんが，英語の名詞は数えられる名詞（複数形をもつ名詞）と，数えられない名詞（単数形だけでしか使われない名詞）に区分されます．次の例に注意しましょう．

[数えられる名詞] a spoon, a book, a pencil, an apple, a chair, a dog, a man, an idea, … /（種類を言う場合）a liquid, a gas, a metal, …

[数えられない名詞]　　some ice cream, some sugar, some tea, some coffee,
　　　　　　　　　　some bread, some ice, some furniture, some fruit, …

　a（**an**）は数を示す不定冠詞（indefinite article）で，単数の数えられる名詞とともに用います．**some** は数や量を示す限定詞（determiner）で，数えられない名詞にも複数形の数えられる名詞にも用います．

　　a. I want *a* Japanese book.（日本語の本がほしい）
　　b. I want *some* Japanese books.（日本語の本が何冊かほしい）
　　c. I want *some* sugar.（砂糖がほしい）
　　d. I want *some* ice cream.（アイスクリームがほしい）
　　e. I need *a* spoon.（スプーンがほしい）

　特定されているものを指示する場合には，a や some のかわりに定冠詞の the を使います．

　　a. I want *the* book.（その本がほしい）
　　b. I want *the* books.（その本がほしい）
　　c. I want *the* sugar.（その砂糖がほしい）
　　d. I want *the* ice cream.（そのアイスクリームがほしい）
　　e. I need *the* spoon.（そのスプーンがほしい）

　特に数や量のことに関係なく一般的に言うときには，次のように some を省きます．

　　a. 数えられる名詞（複数形）
　　　I want some books.　　　　I like *books*.
　　　（何か本がほしい）　　　　（本というものが好きだ）
　　b. 数えられない名詞
　　　I want some sugar.　　　　I like *sugar*.
　　　（砂糖がほしい）　　　　　（砂糖というものが好きだ）

「多少の」という意味を表わす場合，数えられない名詞には **a little** を用い，**a few** は数えられる名詞に用います．

a. I'd like *a little* cream. (少しクリームがほしい)

b. We bought *a few* books. (少し本を買った)

any は否定の叙述文や疑問文でも用います．

a. I have some sugar. (砂糖を持っている)

I don't have *any* sugar. (砂糖を持っていない)

b. He bought some books. (彼は何冊か本を買った)

He didn't buy *any* books. (彼は本を全く買わなかった)

c. Do you want some tea? (お茶はいかが？)

Do you want *any* tea? (お茶ほしいの？)

注意： some 〜 と any 〜 の用法について：some は肯定の叙述文に使われ，疑問文や否定文では any が使われるという説明は誤解の種です．some は疑問文や否定文にも使われます．some は数や量が「いくつ／いくら」の意味が基本です．any は数や量が「どれも／何か；どんな」が基本の意味です．特に any は用いられる範囲について，ものがまったくない場合から無限にある場合を含むことに注意が必要です．any が使われる疑問の意味は「〜がいる／ある／ない」が問われていると考えるとよいでしょう．

3. some, any, one, ones は名詞のかわりに使うことがあります．次の例では，これらの語を省くことはできません．

a. I bought some books. He bought *some*, too.

(私は何冊か本を買った．彼も何冊か買った)

b. I don't want any eggs. She doesn't want *any*, either.

(私は卵はいりません．彼女もいりません)

c. Would you like some tea? — Yes, I'd like *some*.

(お茶をいかが？――はい，いただきます)

d. Would you like some sugar? — No, I don't want *any*.
   (お砂糖をいかが？――いや，けっこうです)
e. He has a book. I have *one*, too.
   (彼は本を持っている．私も持っている)
f. These ties are nice. I like the red *one*.
   (しゃれたネクタイがあるね．私はこの赤いのが好きです)
g. Which apples do you want? — I want the red *ones*.
   (リンゴはどれがいい？――赤いのがいい)

one と ones の用法の違いに注意してください．

a. I want this [that] *one*. I want these [those]. (ones は使わない)
b. I want a blue *one*.　　I want some blue *ones*.
c. I want *one*.　　　　　I want several. (ones は使わない)
　　　　　　　　　　　　I want a few.
　　　　　　　　　　　　I want several big *ones*.
　　　　　　　　　　　　I want a few small *ones*.

4. prefer は「～のほうが好き」にあたります．

a. I *prefer* coffee.（コーヒーのほうが好きだ）
b. I *prefer* to swim.（泳ぐほうが好きだ）

5. What a + 単数の数えられる名詞または **What** + 数えられない名詞または複数の数えられる名詞は感心したり，あきれたりする気持ちを表わすのに使います．

a. What a delicious meal!（ああおいしかった！）
b. What a beautiful tie!（きれいなネクタイね！）
c. What a pity!（何と残念な！）

d. What a waste of time!（何という時間のむだ！）

e. What nice flowers!（きれいな花ですね！）

f. What delicious coffee!（このコーヒーはうまい！）

6. How ＋ 形容詞も感心したり，あきれた気持ちなどを表わすのに使います．

a. How strange!（変ですね！）

b. How expensive!（ああ高い！）

c. How beautiful!（まあきれい！）

d. How disgusting（you are!）（あなたってなんていやな人なの！）

7. アメリカの貨幣

1 dollar（$1.00）＝ 110 yen（as of 2006）

100 cents（100¢）＝ $1.00

5 cents ＝ a nickel

10 cents ＝ a dime

25 cents ＝ a quarter

50 cent ＝ a half dollar

紙幣のことを bill といいます．アメリカの紙幣には現在は次のようなものがあります．かつては 500 ドルから 1 万ドルまで各種の札もありましたが，現在は発行されていません．

1	dollar	bill	20	dollar	bill
2	〃	〃	50	〃	〃
5	〃	〃	100	〃	〃
10	〃	〃			

Lesson Three

Section IV PRONUNCIATION DRILL CD1-11
1. Pronunciation of plural nouns（複数名詞の発音）

Listen and repeat

　a. [ʃ] [tʃ] [s] 以外の無声音で終わる名詞は [s] を添えるだけで複数になります．

　　mat [mæt]　　mats [mæts]　　cake [keik]　　cakes [keiks]
　　cup [kʌp]　　cups [kʌps]　　street [striːt]　　streets [striːts]

　b. [ʒ] [dʒ] [z] 以外の有声音で終わる名詞は [z] を添えるだけで複数になります．

　　egg [eg]　　eggs [egz]　　hand [hænd]　　hands [hændz]
　　dollar [dálɚ]　　dollars [dálɚz]　　apple [ǽpl]　　apples [ǽplz]

　c. [s] [z] [tʃ] [dʒ] [ʃ] [ʒ] で終わる名詞は [iz] を添えて複数にします．
glass [glæs]　　glasses [glǽsiz]　　rose [rouz]　　roses [róuziz]
church [tʃɚtʃ]　　churches [tʃɚ́tʃiz]　　judge [dʒʌdʒ]　　judges [dʒʌ́dʒiz]
dish [diʃ]　　dishes [díʃiz]　　garage [gərɑ́ʒ]　garages [gərɑ́ʒiz]

Exercise: 次の各語を使って文を言いなさい．単数の場合と複数の場合と両方を言いなさい．
　　I didn't see a ＿＿＿. I saw some ＿＿＿.
　　glass, egg, judge, tie, shirt, match, cup, cat, church, hat, dog, dish

2. Pronunciation of *the*（**the** の発音）　the は母音の前では [ði] と発音し，子音の前では [ðə] と発音します．

Listen and repeat

　Exercise: 次の各語を使って文を言いなさい．
　　The ＿＿＿ is here.

apple, bread, cake, ink, egg, table, owl, old man, young woman, name card, money, red ink, extra room, door, oil

3. Pronunciation of *some* (some の発音)　some の発音は弱勢ですが，a certain の意味のときは強勢です．

Listen and repeat

I bought some bread. [ai bɔt səm bred]
（パンを買いました）
Some bread is very expensive. [sʌm bred iz veri ikspensiv]
（パンの中にはとても高価なものがある）

Exercise: 次の各語を使って文を言いなさい．some は弱勢で発音します．

Some ＿＿＿ is on the table.

bread, milk, butter, meat, candy, cake, cheese, flour

上記の各語を使って次の文を言いなさい．some は強勢で発音します．

Some ＿＿＿ is very expensive.

4. Pronunciation of *any* (any の発音)　弱勢の場合の any は否定に使われます．強勢の場合の any は，「どんな〜でも」とか「ちっとも」の意味です．

Listen and repeat

I don't have any books. (私は本を持っていない)
I don't have any books. (私はどんな本も1冊も持っていない)
I like to read any book. (私はどんな本でも読むのが好きだ)

Exercise: 次の各語を使って文を言いなさい．ここでは any は弱勢です．

Did you get any _____?

books, coffee, sugar, shirts, fruit, apples, advice, eggs, pencils, ink, oil, bread

上記の各語を使って次の文を言いなさい．ここでは any は強勢です．

I didn't get any _____.

5. Pronunciation of [uː] and [u] ([uː] と [u] の発音)　[uː] の場合の舌の位置は，日本語の[ウ]に比べると唇をうんとまるめて力を入れて突き出すというところが違います．

Listen and repeat

| you [juː] | knew [njuː] | do [duː] |
| too [tuː] | soup [suːp] | zoo [zuː] |

[u] の場合の唇はいくぶん丸めにするだけです．舌の位置は [uː] の場合よりいくらか低めです．

Listen and repeat

| could [kud] | hood [hud] | would [wud] |
| nook [nuk] | cook [kuk] | soot [sut] |

Exercise: 次の各組の語を使って文を言いなさい．

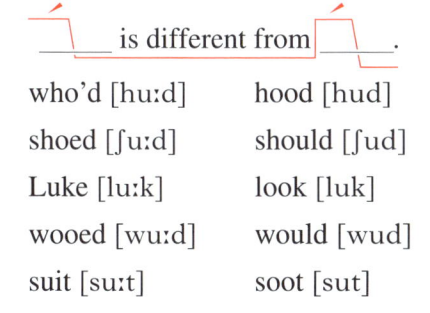

_____ is different from _____.

who'd [huːd]　　hood [hud]
shoed [ʃuːd]　　should [ʃud]
Luke [luːk]　　look [luk]
wooed [wuːd]　　would [wud]
suit [suːt]　　soot [sut]

Section V PATTERN USAGE DRILL CD1-12

Listen and repeat

1. ⇒ Chart I.
    1. I want to play baseball today. Would you like to play, too? / Yes. I'd like to play very much.

    （以下続ける）

2. 例にならい，次の語句を使って問いと答を言いなさい．
    例）Would you like some coffee? / No, thank you. I don't like coffee.
    1. some tea
    2. some orange juice
    3. some cake
    4. some pie
    5. some ice cream
    6. some juice
    7. some wine
    8. some whisky
    9. some fruit
    10. some rice

3. 例にならい，問題2の語句を使って問いと答を言いなさい．
    例）Do you like tea? / Yes. I like tea very much. I'd like some now.

4. ⇒ Chart II. チャートの内容によくなじむまで練習しなさい．
    1. I have a pen and some paper.
    2. I have a knife and some fruit.
    3. I have a doughnut and some coffee.
    4. I have a toothbrush and some toothpaste.
    5. I have an egg and some bacon.
    6. I have a spoon and some ice cream.
    7. I have a watch and some furniture.

Lesson Three

   8. I have a ring and some perfume.
   9. I have a glass and some juice.

5. ⇒ Chart II.
   1. Would you like a pen? / Yes. I'd like one. I'd like some paper, too. Do you have any? / Yes. I have some.

   (以下続ける)

6. 例にならい，次の語句を使って，I'd like ～. および I don't want ～. の文を言いなさい．
   例) I'd like an apple. (fruit) / I'd like some fruit. (don't want) / I don't want any fruit. (apple) / I don't want an apple.
   1. coffee
   2. ice cream
   3. tea
   4. cookie
   5. furniture
   6. ties
   7. textbook
   8. notebooks
   9. shirt
   10. juice
   11. gifts
   12. tie

7. 例にならい，次の語句を使って問いと答を言いなさい．
   例) Do you want an apple? / No. I don't want an apple. / Oh? Why not? / I don't like apples.
   Do you want some juice? / No. I don't want any juice. / Oh? Why not? / I don't like juice.
   1. a peach
   2. some fruit
   3. some tea
   4. a cookie
   5. some sugar
   6. a pear
   7. some ice coffee
   8. an orange
   9. some ice cream
   10. some wine

49

8. 例にならい，問題7の語句を使って対話を完成しなさい．

例) I'd like an apple. / I'd like one, too.
I'd like some juice. / I'd like some, too.

9. 例にならい，問題7の語句を使って対話を完成しなさい．

例) I didn't buy an apple. Did you buy one? / No. I didn't buy one.
I didn't buy any juice. Did you buy any? / No. I didn't buy any.

10. 次の＿＿の部分に必要な場合には some, any, a (an) を入れなさい．ただし，答は一通りとは限りません．

1. Would you like ＿＿ tea?
2. Do you want ＿＿ orange juice?
3. I like ＿＿ movies.
4. I don't want ＿＿ juice.
5. I prefer ＿＿ blue shirt.
6. I prefer ＿＿ red tie.
7. I bought ＿＿ ice cream.
8. I don't like ＿＿ blue sport shirts.
9. We used ＿＿ American money.
10. We saw ＿＿ American dollars.
11. We didn't see ＿＿ American movies.
12. We like ＿＿ American movies.

11. 例にならい，問題7の語句を使って対話を完成しなさい．

例) I bought a few apples. / Oh? I bought a few, too.
I bought a little juice. / Oh? I bought a little, too.

Lesson Three

12. ⇒ Chart II.
1. These pens are nice. I like the red one.
2. These knives are nice. I like the big one.
3. These doughnuts are nice. I like the chocolate one.
4. plastic
5. 省く.
6. silver
7. gold
8. silver
9. brown

13. ⇒ Chart II.
1. What an expensive pen! What beautiful paper!
2. What a good knife! What delicious fruit!
3. delicious/hot
4. cheap/good
5. delicious/delicious
6. nice/rich
7. old/modern
8. expensive/old
9. useful/good

14. ⇒ Chart II.
1. Do you want the pen or the paper? / I prefer the pen.
（以下続ける）

15. 例にならい，次の語句を使って問いと答を言いなさい．
例) Did you buy a pen or a knife? / I bought a knife.
1. a sport shirt / a dress shirt
2. some fruit / some cake
3. some candy / some ice cream
4. some furniture / some pictures
5. a watch / a diamond ring
6. a blue tie / a red tie

7. a red shirt / a white shirt
8. some A4 paper / some blue ink
9. some old furniture / some modern furniture
10. some apples / some pears

16. ⇒ Chart II.
1. Do you want some pens? / No, I don't want any.
   Do you want some paper? / No, I don't want any.
（以下続ける）

17. ⇒ Chart II.
1. He doesn't have any pens, but he wants some.
   He doesn't have any paper, but he wants some.
（以下続ける）

18. ⇒ Chart II.
1. I don't have a pen, but I'd like one.
   I don't have any paper, but I'd like some.
（以下続ける）

19. 例にならい，対話を完成しなさい．
  例) Here are some pens. Would you like one? / Yes, thank you. I'd like one. / All right. Here you are.

1. some sport shirts
2. some oranges
3. some pears
4. some peaches
5. some apples
6. some belts
7. some nice ties
8. some pictures
9. some pencils
10. some dictionaries

20. ⇒ Chart II.
1. I have an old pen, but you have some new ones.
   I have some typing paper, but you have some writing paper.
2. I have a good knife, but you have a dull one.
   I have some expensive fruit, but you have some cheap fruit.
3. fresh/stale   hot/ice
4. wooden/plastic   expensive/cheap
5. fried/boiled   fried/raw
6. silver/plastic   chocolate/vanilla
7. gold/silver   old/new
8. gold/silver   old/new
9. brown/white   fresh/canned

21. 次の話を読み，問いに答えなさい．

　Mary had a delicious meal this evening. She doesn't want any coffee. She prefers tea. She doesn't use sugar in her tea. Her friend Jane uses a little sugar and a little cream. Mary'd like some fruit now. She'd like an apple. Fruit is very cheap now. Apples are only one dollar a pound. Mary'd like a glass of water now. She doesn't like juice. Jane doesn't want any water. She prefers juice.
1. Did Mary eat today?
2. When?
3. Does she want any coffee?
4. Why not?
5. Does she use sugar in her tea?
6. Does Jane?
7. Does Mary want some fruit?

8. What kind?
9. Does Mary like juice?
10. Does Jane?

22. 下線の部分に適切な語句を入れなさい.

A: I just baked a fresh _____, would you like some?
B: No, thank you. I don't want _____ cake.

A: Can I bring you some _____?
B: Yes, please. _____ like some water.

A: I just bought some apples, would you like _____?
B: No, thank you. I just ate a banana, I don't want _____ apples.

A: Do you _____ my white dress or the black one?
B: I like the black one _____.

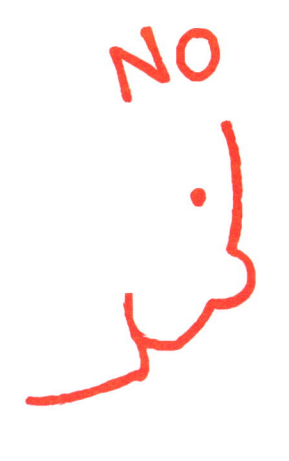

Lesson Four
WHAT DID YOU DO TODAY?
今日は何をしましたか

Section I Presentation CD1-13

Two friends share information about each other's day. The friends show their interest by asking questions. They don't agree on everything, but they are still good friends.

友人同士互いに一日のさまざまなことを共有します．いろいろ尋ねることで相互の関心をはっきり示します．何事にも2人が一致するということはありません．でも2人は良き友人なのです．

Section II Application dialogue CD1-14

Listen and repeat

A I went shopping today.
B Oh? What did you buy?

今日は買物に行ってきました．
そうですか．何を買ったのですか．

A	Not much. I just bought some clothes—a few shirts and some ties.	たいした買物ではありません．衣類を少し買っただけです．——ワイシャツ数枚とネクタイ 2, 3 本です．
B	Where did you go?	どこへ行ったのですか．
A	To the department store. It's very convenient.	デパートです．デパートはとても便利です．
B	I like to shop at the department store, too.	私もよくデパートで買物をします．
A	What did you do today?	あなたは今日何をしましたか．
B	I played tennis in the morning. In the afternoon I went to the movies.	午前中はテニスをやりました．午後は映画を見に行きました．
A	Where did you play tennis?	テニスはどこでやりましたか．
B	Well, I wanted to play in the park, but it was too crowded. So I went to my company's courts.	それがですね，公園でやりたいと思ったのですが，とても混んでいたのです．それで私の会社のコートへ行きました．
A	Oh? Where are they located?[1]	そうですか．それはどこにあるのですか．
B	In the countryside. Near Springville.	いなかです．スプリングビルの近くです．
A	How long does it take to get there?	そこへはどのくらい時間がかかるのですか．
B	It just takes an hour.	ほんの 1 時間です．
A	Did you go by train?	列車で行ったのですか．
B	No. There's no train to Springville.	いいえ，スプリングビル行きの列車はありません．
A	How did you go, then?	では，どうやって行ったのですか．
B	I went by bus. I came back at about two o'clock and went to the movies.	バスで行きました．2 時ごろ戻ってきて映画を見に行きました．
A	What kind of a movie did you see?	どんな映画を見たのですか．

---

1) **be located** 〜 〜にある．

Lesson Four

B I saw a Western. It was very exciting.
A I don't like Westerns. They're all the same.
B What kind of movies do you like?
A Romantic ones.
B Romantic movies are all the same, too. I prefer Westerns.

西部劇を見ました．見ていてとてもハラハラするような映画でした．
西部劇は好きではありません．どれも同じですからね．
どんな映画が好きですか．
ロマンチックなのがいいです．
ロマンチックな映画だってどれも同じでしょう．私は西部劇のほうが好きです．

Section III NOTES ON CONVERSATIONAL STYLE

1. do, does または did の前に疑問詞をつけて作る疑問文は，次のようになります．

   You bought a book.
   Did you *buy* a book?　　〈疑問のしるしとして Did を使う〉
  What did you buy?　　〈a book を what に換える〉

疑問詞が疑問文のはじめにくることに注意してください．次に示すのは疑問詞を使った問いとその答の例です．

a. *What* did you buy? — A book.
b. *What* did you do today? — I played tennis.
c. *What* kind of fruit do you like? — I like apples.
d. *When* does he skate? — On Saturday.
e. *Where* did they go? — To the park.
f. *Why* did she go to the bookstore? — To get some books.
g. *How* do you feel? — Very well, thank you.
h. *How* long did you play tennis? — For two hours.

i. *Which* tie do you want? — The red one.

2. just は run, walk, buy などの動詞にはそのすぐ前に使います．be, can, might, should などの場合には，そのすぐ後にきます．

  a. I *just* came home.（私は今帰ってきたばかりだ）
  b. I *just* want an apple.（リンゴだけがほしい）
  c. He is *just* a child.（彼はほんの子供だ）
  d. You should *just* study harder.（ただもっと勉強すればいいのだ）

3. go + ～ing（～(し)に行く）は，次のような場合に用います．

  a. I *went* shopp*ing* yesterday.（買物に行く）
  b. He likes to *go* swimm*ing*.（泳ぎに行く）
  c. We *go* hik*ing* every summer.（ハイキングに行く）
  d. Did you *go* skat*ing*?（スケートに行く）
  e. We didn't *go* fish*ing*.（魚釣りに行く）
  f. I like to *go* golf*ing*.
  g. Do you want to *go* bowl*ing*?
  h. They *went* jogg*ing*.
  i. We *went* cycl*ing* yesterday.
  j. They want to *go* mountain climb*ing*.

しかし，野球，フットボール，テニス，ラグビー，バスケットボール，バレーボールなどのような球技には go + ～ing の形は用いません．

  a. We played baseball. We didn't play football.
  b. Do you like to play tennis? No. I like to play rugby.

Lesson Four

▌ **4. in the morning, last year, next week** というように時間を表わす語句は文末におきますが，さらに時間を表わす語句が続く場合には時間の継続性を保つためそれを文のはじめに置くこともあります．

　　a. I played tennis *in the morning*. *In the afternoon* I went to the movies.
　　b. We went to Kyoto *last week*. *This week* we went to Sendai.

▌ **5. by**（時に **on**）を使って，交通や通信手段について言う場合には the をつけることもあります．

　　a. We didn't go by train. / We went by bus. / I wanted to go by bike. / They came by taxi. / We want to go to Japan by boat.[1] / We don't want to go by plane. / He goes to work by bus. / He doesn't go by train.
　　b. We talked by telephone. / We talked on *the* telephone. / I spoke to him by *the* Internet. / I heard him over *the* radio.
　　c. I saw the show on television.
　　d. I saw your picture in *the* newspaper.

Section IV PRONUNCIATION DRILL　CD1-15

▌ **1. Pronunciation of** [ɑ] **and** [ɔ]（[ɑ] と [ɔ] の発音）　[ɑ] は日本語の[ア]と似ていますが，日本語の場合よりもっとあごを開きます．あくびをするときの[ア]と考えればよいでしょう．

---

1) boat と ship の区別: 海事専門用語としては boat は「救命ボートなど，他の船に乗せられる小さな船」で，ship は「他の船に乗せられないほど大きな船」ですが，一般用語としては boat = ship です．アメリカ英語の口語では ship より boat を好んで使います．

[ɔ] は，卵を太いほうを先にして口の中へ全部入れたようなつもりで発音すると，うまくゆきます．また [ɔ] では，唇をまるめて突き出すことがたいせつです．ただし，[ɑ] も [ɔ] もやや長めに発音するつもりで言ってください．

Listen and repeat

cot [kɑt]	caught [kɔt]
not [nɑt]	nought [nɔt]
sot [sɑt]	sought [sɔt]
pa [pɑ]	paw [pɔ]
cock [kɑk]	caulk [kɔk]
tot [tɑt]	taught [tɔt]
don [dɑn]	dawn [dɔn]

Exercise: 上記の語を使って，次の文を言いなさい．

How do you spell _____?

2. Pronunciation of [ɚ]（[ɚ] の発音）　[ɚ] は [r] の発音とまったく同じです．図のように，舌先を上へ持ち上げ，スプーンのような形にします．このとき，舌先はどこにもついてはいけません．唇の形は，日本語で言えば，[ウ]と言うときとほとんど同じです．[ア]ほどにあごを開いてはいけません．[ɚ] は [r] と同じだと言いましたが，それは，この音が母音にも子音にも使われるからです．母音として使うときは [ɚ]，子音のときは [r] と書いて区別するわけです．

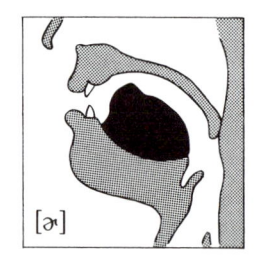

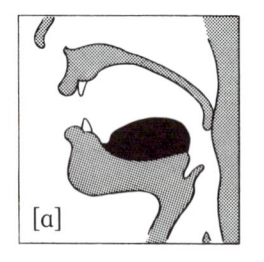

[ɚ]　　[ɑ]

Listen and repeat

hot [hɑt]	hurt [hɚt]
dot [dɑt]	dirt [dɚt]
cot [cɑt]	curt [kɚt]
shot [ʃɑt]	shirt [ʃɚt]
lock [lɑk]	lurk [lɚk]
pot [pɑt]	pert [pɚt]
god [gɑd]	gird [gɚd]

Exercise: 上記の各語を下の＿＿＿の部分に入れて発音してみなさい．

Did you say ＿＿＿ or ＿＿＿ ?

3. 母音の前の [t] は，しばしば [d] と発音します．[d] の前の [t] は，しばしば聞こえません．

Listen and repeat

butter [bʌdɚ]　　　Betty [bédi]

water [wɔ́dɚ]　　　cutter [kʌ́dɚ]

What are you? [(h)wəd ɚ juː]

Put it there. [pud it ðer]

It ate some bread. [id éit səm bréd]

What do you want? [wə də ju wánt]

What did you do today? [wə did ju dúː tədei]

What did he do? [wə didi dúː]

Section V PATTERN USAGE DRILL CD1-16

Listen and repeat

1. 例にならい，次の語句を使って，I went 〜. I played 〜. の文を言いなさい．
   例) I went shopping today. (fish) ⇒ I went fishing today. (*shogi*) ⇒ I played *shogi* today. (tennis) I played tennis today. (skate) ⇒ I went skating today.
   1. baseball
   2. golf
   3. soccer
   4. swim
   5. volleyball
   6. ski
   7. surf
   8. sightsee
   9. rugby
   10. football

2. 例にならい，問題1の各語を使って問いと答を言いなさい．
   例) Did you go shopping today? / No. I didn't go shopping. I went fishing.
   Did you go fishing today? / No. I didn't go fishing. I played *shogi*.
   Did you play *shogi* today? / No. I didn't play *shogi*. I played tennis.

3. 学習者にきのう何をしたか尋ね，めいめいに答えさせなさい．
   例) What did you do yesterday? / I went surfing.

4. ⇒ Chart I.
   1. What did you do today? / I played baseball.

   （以下続ける）

5. ⇒ Chart II.
   1. want / What did he want? / He wanted a pen and some paper.
   2. buy / What did he buy? / He bought a knife and some fruit.
   3. order   6. ask for   8. want
   4. need   7. want   9. ask for
   5. eat

6. 例にならい，次の文を What で始まる疑問文にしなさい．
   例) I bought a book. / What did you buy?
       I like juice. / What do you like?
       She wants to play tennis. / What does she want to play?
   1. I bought some clothes.
   2. Professor McCarthy teaches English.
   3. I saw an exciting movie.
   4. I like Westerns.
   5. I wanted to buy some shoes.
   6. I'd like an apple.
   7. She has to buy a new skirt.
   8. He wants some ties.
   9. She asked for some money.
   10. She needs a watch.

7. ⇒ Chart I.
   1. (Bob) ⇒ What does Bob want to do today? / He wants to play baseball.
   2. Harry   5. he   8. he
   3. you   6. you   9. he
   4. they   7. Sachiko

8. ⇒ Chart II.
1. (you, buy) ⇒ What did you buy yesterday? / I bought a pen and some paper.
2. he, buy
3. they, order
4. you, need
5. she, eat
6. he, ask for
7. you, buy
8. she, want
9. he, ask for

9. Chart III を使って，内容によく慣れるまで練習しなさい．
1. Bill went to Oshima by boat.
2. Sachiko went to the zoo by bus.
3. Peggy talked to Ann by phone.
4. Mr. Fox saw the show on television.
5. Haruko went to the movie theater by taxi.
6. Mike went to the mountains by bike.
7. Mrs. Cleveland went to the United States by plane.
8. Eddie and Sue went to the countryside by train.
9. Harry went to the lake by horse.

10. ⇒ Chart III.
1. How did Bill go to Oshima? / He went by boat.
2. How did Sachiko go to the zoo? / She went by bus.
3. How did Peggy talk to Ann? / She talked by phone.
4. How did Mr. Fox see the show? / He saw it on television.
5. How did Haruko go to the movie theater [house]? / She went by taxi.
6. How did Mike go to the mountains? / He went by bike.
7. How did Mrs. Cleveland go to the United States? / She went by plane.

8. How did Eddie and Sue go to the countryside? / They went by train.
9. How did Harry go to the lake? / He went by horse.

11. ⇒ Chart III.
    1. Where / Where did Bill go? / He went to Oshima.
    2. What / What did Sachiko do? / She went to the zoo.
    3. What   6. Where   9. What
    4. What   7. Where
    5. Where   8. Where

12. ⇒ Chart III.
    1. What did Bill have to do? / He had to go to Oshima.
    （以下続ける）

13. ⇒ Chart I.
    1. Where does Bob play baseball? / He plays in the park.
    2. Where does Harry work? / He works at the bookstore.
    （以下続ける）

14. ⇒ Chart I.
    1. Where did you go yesterday? / I went to the park. / What did you do? / I played baseball.
    2. Where did you go yesterday? / I went to the bookstore. / What did you do? / I worked.
    （以下続ける）

15. 例にならい，次の語句を使って(　)の語を変えながら会話練習をしなさい (a few の後には複数の数えられる名詞を，a little の後には数えられない名詞を使うこと).

 例) —What did you do today?

  —I went shopping.

  —Oh? What did you buy?

  —Not much. I just bought a few (shirts) and a little (fruit).

 1. a few books / a little paper

 2. a few curtains / a little furniture

 3. a few doughnuts / a little candy

 4. a few CDs / a little coffee

16. ⇒ Chart III.

 1. When did Bill go to Oshima? / He went last month. / Does he go every month? / No, he doesn't.

 2. When did Sachiko go to the zoo? / She went last week. / Does she go every week? / No, she doesn't.

 3. last night 6. last May 9. last fall

 4. last night 7. last summer

 5. last Sunday 8. last spring

17. 例にならい，(　)内の語を適当に変えながら，会話練習をしなさい．

 例) —What did you do today?

  —I (played tennis) in the morning. In the afternoon I (played chess).

18. 例にならい，住所についての会話練習をしなさい．

 例) —Where do you live?

  —I live in Senzoku.

—Oh? Where's it located?
—In Tokyo. In Meguro Ward.

—Where do you live?
—I live in Atami.
—Oh? Where's it located?
—In Shizuoka Prefecture. Near Hakone.

19. 例にならい，仕事先を尋ねる会話練習をしなさい．

例) —Where do you work?
—At the Mitsutomo Bank.
—Oh? Where's it located?
—In Tokyo. Near Nihonbashi.

—Where do you work?
—At the Isemaru Department Store.
—Oh? Where's it located?
—In Nagoya. Near Sakae-machi.

20. ⇒ Chart III.
1. How long does it take to get to Oshima? / It takes about three hours.
2. the zoo / about twenty minutes
3. Peggy's house / about ten minutes
4. Mr. Fox's house / about an hour
5. the movie theater [house] / about fifteen minutes
6. the mountains / about four hours
7. the United States / about ten hours

8. the countryside / about two hours
9. the lake / about forty minutes

21. 例にならい，会話練習をしなさい．

   例) —Where do you live?
   —I live in Hachioji.
   —How long does it take to get there?
   —It takes about an hour.

   —Where do you live?
   —I live in Shibuya.
   —How long does it take to get there?
   —It takes about twenty-five minutes.

22. 例にならい，会話練習をしなさい．

   例) —I live in Aoyama. It takes about twenty minutes to get there.
   —Do you go by train?
   —No, there's no train to Aoyama.
   —How do you go, then?
   —I go by bus.

   —I live in Kami-machi. It takes about two hours to get there.
   —Do you go by subway?
   —No, there's no subway to Kami-machi.
   —How do you go, then?
   —I go by bus.

23. ⇒ Chart II.
1. What kind of pen did you buy? / I bought a cheap one.
   What kind of paper did you buy? / I bought some writing paper.
2. a small one / some apples
3. a chocolate one / some instant coffee
4. a plastic one / some cheap toothpaste
5. a boiled one / some Swiss cheese
6. a silver one / some vanilla ice cream
7. a gold watch / some modern furniture
8. a silver one / some French perfume.
9. a brown one / some fruit juice

24. 例にならい，次の語を使って会話練習をしなさい．
例) —What kind of movies do you like?
　　—I like romantic ones. What kind do you like?
　　—I like thrillers.

　　—What kind of fruit do you like?
　　—I like peaches. What kind do you like?
　　—I like apples.

1. sports
2. video games
3. magazines
4. food
5. clothes
6. books
7. TV programs
8. computers
9. juice
10. tea

25. ⇒ Chart I.
　　1. Why did Dick go to the park? / He went to the park to play baseball.
　（以下続ける）

26. ⇒ Chart II.
　　1. Which did you want, the pen or the paper? / I just wanted the pen. I didn't need the paper.
　　2. buy　　4. need　　6. ask for　　8. ask for
　　3. order　5. eat　　　7. buy　　　9. need

27. 次の問いに答えなさい．
　　1. Where did you go yesterday?
　　2. When did you come here today?
　　3. What did you do this morning?
　　4. What did you eat at noon?
　　5. What do you want to do tonight?
　　6. What kind of fruit do you like?
　　7. Why do you want to study English?
　　8. How long do you study English every day?
　　9. How long does it take to get to your house?
　　10. What kind of movies do you like?

28. 学習者が先生に質問をしてみなさい．
　例) Where do you live?
　　　What kind of books do you like?
　　　When did you come to Japan?

29. 下線の部分に適切な語句を入れなさい．

A: _____ did you go yesterday?
B: _____ the department store.

A: _____ did you buy for the trip?
B: I bought a _____ sandwiches and some drinks.

A: How long will it take _____ to get there?
B: It'll take _____ hour.

A: What _____ of a hotel will we stay at?
B: It's a Japanese _____ hotel, a *ryokan*.

Lesson Five
WHAT'S YOUR NAME?
お名前は

Section I PRESENTATION CD1-17

A staff member asks a student some questions. These questions are personal, but in this case it is acceptable. The staff member asks him "What's your name?" This question is very "official." A more friendly way to ask this question is; "May I have your name (please)?"

学校の事務職員は学生に必要な質問をします。これらの質問は個人に係わる内容です。しかしこの場合はやむを得ないことです。職員が学生に「名前は？」と尋ねます。この質問は極めてそっけない事務的なものです。名前の聞き方でもっと親しみのある尋ね方は、「お名前を（どうぞ）教えてください」です。

Lesson Five

Section II APPLICATION DIALOGUE CD1-18

Listen and repeat

A　Excuse me. I'd like to register[1] for the fall classes.[2]

B　Yes, of course.[3] What's your name?

A　My name is William Cleveland.

B　Were you a student here last semester?[4]

A　Yes, I was. Do I have to fill in a new registration card?

B　Yes. We need a new card every semester. What's your address?

A　1964 Superior Avenue. I'm living there with my parents now. But I want to find a room near the university.

B　Oh? I know a nice room on Green Street.

A　Is it expensive?

B　No, it isn't. It's very cheap.

A　Is it in a hotel or something?

失礼します．秋のクラスに登録したいのですが．

はい，どうぞ．お名前は？

ウィリアム・クリーブランドといいます．

この前の学期もここの学生でしたか．

ええ，そうです．新しい登録カードに書きこまなくてはいけませんか．

そうです．学期ごとに新しく登録していただくことになっています．ご住所は？

スペリアー街の1964番地です．そこに今両親といっしょに住んでいます．でも大学の近くに部屋を見つけたいと思っています．

そうですか．グリーン通りに，いい部屋を知ってますよ．

高いでしょうか．

いいえ，とても安いですよ．

そこはホテルか何かですか．

---

1) **register** ここでは「受講の手続きをする」．
2) **fall classes** 秋の授業，または講習．fall《米》= autumn.
3) **of course** 相手の求めに応じていねいに答える言い方．「どうぞどうぞ」の意味．
4) **semester** [səméstɚ]（米国の）学期．たとえば2学期制の学校では，fall semester（9月から1月の中ごろまで）と spring semester（2月より6月の中ごろまで）の2つにわかれている．

B No, it isn't. It's in Professor McCarthy's home. / いいえ、そうではなくて、マッカーシー教授のお宅です。

A Isn't he an English professor? / その方は英語の教授ではありませんか。

B Yes, he is. Were you one of his students? / ええ、そうです。授業をうけたことがありますか。

A Yes, I was. I was in his class last year. / ええ、あります。昨年その先生のクラスにいました。

B Do you know his wife? / あの方の奥さんを知っていますか。

A No. Is she a teacher, too? / いいえ、奥さんも先生ですか。

B Yes. She teaches music. She's very interesting. Professor McCarthy and his wife are very nice. Would you like to see the room? / ええ、音楽を教えておられます。とてもいい方です。ご夫妻とも、とてもすてきな方です。お部屋をごらんになりたいですか。

A Yes, I would. / ええ、お願いします。

B Here's their address. 264 Green Street. Professor McCarthy is at home now. He's painting his living room. / はい、これがその住所です。グリーン通りの264番地です。マッカーシー教授は今在宅しておられます。居間のペンキを塗っておられますよ。

A Fine. I want to see the room now. Thanks for your advice. / それはよかった。これから部屋を見に行きたいと思います。お心づかいありがとうございました。

B You're welcome. / どういたしまして。

Section III NOTES ON CONVERSATIONAL STYLE

1. be 動詞（am, are, was, were）を含む文を疑問文にするには be 動詞を主語の前に置きます。

　　a. You are a student. → *Are* you a student?

Yes, I am. / No, I'm not.
- b. He is a doctor. → *Is* he a doctor?
  Yes, he is. / No, he isn't.
- c. She was a nurse. → *Was* she a nurse?
  Yes, she was. / No, she wasn't.
- d. They were students. → *Were* they students?
  Yes, they were. / No, they weren't.

2. be 動詞の否定には次のように 2 つの形があります (ただし I am の場合は 1 つだけ)

- a. I'm a student.　　I'*m not* a student.
- b. You're a doctor.　You'*re not* a doctor.
  　　　　　　　　　You *aren't* a doctor.
- c. He's a teacher.　　He'*s not* a teacher.
  　　　　　　　　　He *isn't* a teacher.
- d. We're students.　　We'*re not* students.
  　　　　　　　　　We *aren't* students.

この 2 つの形はどちらを使ってもよく，意味は大して変わりません．

3. 疑問詞を主語にして be 動詞を含む文を疑問文にするとき，疑問詞を主語の位置に置きます．

- a. *He* is a doctor. → *Who* is a doctor?
- b. *The book* is there. → *What*'s there?
- c. *This man* is a teacher. → *Which man* is a teacher?

4. be + 動詞の 〜ing 形は，今行われている動作を表わすときに使います．

'be + 動詞の 〜ing 形' と現在形との意味上のちがいを次の例文で確かめてください．

    a. I *play* tennis every day.〈毎日やる——習慣です〉

        I *am playing* tennis now.〈今やっている——ところです〉

    b. We *study* in the evening.〈夜にする——習慣です〉

        We *are studying* now.〈今している——ところです〉

5. 動作が含まれていなければ 〜ing 形は必要ではありません．be 動詞, like, have, own, belong to, know, understand などがよく使われる**状態を表わす動詞**です．

    a. I *have* a small car.（私は小さな車を持っています）

    b. She *belongs* to the sports club.（彼女はスポーツクラブにはいっています）

    c. He *is* a doctor.（彼は医者です）

    d. I *know* a nice internet café.（いいネットカフェを知っています）

状態の意味のときは動詞を be + 〜ing 形で使うのは誤りです．

    Right: I have a car. / She belongs to the club.

    Wrong: I *am having* a car. / She *is belonging* to the club.

6. be + 〜ing 形の疑問文は主語と be 動詞を置き換えて作ります．

    a. You are playing tennis now. → *Are* you playing tennis now?

    b. He is watching a movie. → *Is* he watching a movie?

7. 形容詞は修飾する語の前に置きますが，（前置詞に導かれる）**形容詞句**は，修飾される語の後にきます．また**分詞形容詞**（〜ing, -ed, 不規則な過去分詞）も修飾される語の後にくることがあります．

a. The *red* book is mine.
   The book *on the table* is mine.
   The *tall* man is a doctor.
   The man *near the window* is a doctor.
   I know a *nice* room *on Green Street*.
b. The *tall* boys are students.
   The boys *singing in the street* are students.
   The *red-haired* girl is my sister.
   The girl *playing the piano* is my sister.
c. The book *placed on the table* is mine.
   That *large* picture was painted last year.
   The picture *painted last year* was sold yesterday.

8. 〜 or something これは「〜か何か」「〜のようなもの」などの意味を表わす言い方です．

a. I read it in a book *or something*.
   （そのことは本か何かで読みました）
b. My sister has the flu *or something*.
   （妹は流感か何かにかかっています）
c. I think he's a doctor *or something*.
   （彼は医者か何かだと思います）

Section IV PRONUNCIATION DRILL　CD1-19

1. Pronunciation of [l]　([l] の発音)　舌の先を上の前歯の裏側にあてて，舌で歯をおさえて[ウ]のような音を出せば，それが[l]です．舌の先を口の内部に向けて曲げないように注意してください．舌の先は上歯の裏側にあたっているのです．

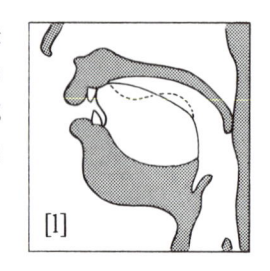

Listen and repeat

　　[ku: l ku: l ku:l] cool　　[pi: l pi: l pi:l] peel

　[l] の音は，舌の先を上の前歯にあてて，前の母音の有声音を続ければできます．その場合，息は舌の両側からぬけて行きます．

Listen and repeat

　　[l i:p l i:p li:p] leap　　[l eit l eit leit] late
　　[gʌ l gʌ l gʌl] gull　　[gi l gi l gil] gill

2. Pronunciation of [r]　([r] の発音)　日本語では [r] の音と [l] の音を区別しません．日本語の「たたいて出す r 音」は舌の先で口蓋をすばやくたたくと同時に有声音を出すと出ます．すでにおわかりのように，英語の [l] は舌を上の前歯にあてて出すのですが，英語の [r] は右の図のように口の中で舌の先をうしろに曲げて出すのです．この音は日本の学習者にはひどくむずかしいようで，[r] の音を出そうとすると，どうしても舌の先で口蓋をたたいてしまいがちです．右の図解のように舌の先をうしろへカールさせて，有声音を出すと，[r] の音が出るのです．なお，Lesson 4 で説明したように，[r] は [ɚ] と同じです．

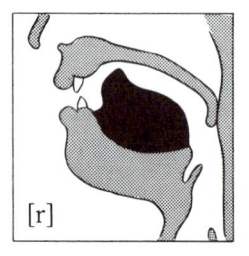

Lesson Five

3. Contrast between [l] and [r]（[l] と [r] との対比）

Listen and repeat

1. pill [pil]　　　peer [pir][1)]
2. bell [bel]　　　bear [ber]
3. tell [tel]　　　tear [ter]
4. fill [fil]　　　fear [fir]
5. ill [il]　　　ear [ir]

6. led [led]　　　red [red]
7. late [leit]　　　rate [reit]
8. light [lait]　　　write [rait]
9. lead [liːd]　　　read [riːd]
10. lent [lent]　　　rent [rent]

11. glass [glæs]　　　grass [græs]
12. glean [gliːn]　　　green [griːn]
13. clown [klaun]　　　crown [kraun]
14. play [plei]　　　pray [prei]
15. bleed [bliːd]　　　breed [briːd]

16. [ðə rais iz pritiː hɑt]
17. [piːl ə per pliːz]
18. [niːl daun nir ðə bel]
19. [ail wɑnt ə dil pikl təmɑrə]

1）辞書には，[piɚ] [peɚ] [teɚ] [fiɚ]　局同じことです。
　　[iɚ] と表記したものもありますが，結

79

20. [tɚn an ðe lait bət dount rait]
21. [dount prei bifɔr ðe grei bel]
22. [trai ðis glæs its veri gud]

Exercise: 次の各語を使って文を言いなさい．

Look at the _____ .

bells, bears, pears, clowns, crowns, rice, grass, glass

4. be 動詞を含む疑問文の読み方は，ふつう 2–3 抑揚パターンを用います．

Listen and repeat

1. Were you a student here before?
2. Is it in a hotel or something?
3. Is she a teacher, too?
4. Was he in the professor's class?
5. Am I a good student?
6. Are you a doctor?

---

16. The rice is pretty hot.
17. Peel a pear please.
18. Kneel down near the bell.
19. I'll want a dill pickle tomorrow.
20. Turn on the light but don't write.
21. Don't pray before the gray bell.
22. Try this glass. It's very good.   (pp. 79–80)

Lesson Five

Section V PATTERN USAGE DRILL CD1-20

Listen and repeat

1. ⇒ Chart IV. チャートの内容によくなじむまで練習しなさい.

1. Jennie's very happy now.
2. Jimmy's very sad now.
3. Mr. Cleveland's very tired now.
4. Hanako's very hungry now.
5. Mr. Johnson's very calm now.
6. George's very busy now.
7. William's very thirsty now.
8. Marilyn's very sleepy now.
9. Dick's very sick now.

2. ⇒ Chart IV.

1. I / I'm very happy now.
   you / You're very happy now.
   she / She's very happy now.
   we / We're very happy now.
   they / They're very happy now.

（以下続ける）

3. ⇒ Chart II.

1. This is my pen. It's new.
   That's my paper. It's A4 size.
2. This is my knife. It's sharp.
   That's my fruit. It's delicious.

（いろいろな形容詞を使って続ける）

4. 例にならい，次の語を使って順番に換えなさい．

例) We're very busy now. (She) / She's very busy now.
(You) / You're very busy now. (late) / You're very late now.

1. I	6. surprised	11. Fruit
2. We	7. We	12. Melons
3. He	8. I	13. It
4. early	9. They	14. sweet
5. excited	10. expensive	15. hot

5. ⇒ Chart IV.
1. What's your name? / My name is Jennie. / How do you spell it? / J-e-n-n-i-e.
2. What's his name? / His name is Jimmy. / How do you spell it? / J-i-m-m-y.

（以下続ける）

6. 例にならい，下の語句を使って会話練習をしなさい．

例) —Excuse me. I'd like to register for the fall classes.
—Yes, of course. What's your name?
—My name is Tomiko Shimizu.
—How do you spell it?
—T-o-m-i-k-o S-h-i-m-i-z-u.
—Thank you.

1. the summer classes
2. the fall semester
3. the English conversation class
4. the music class
5. the American literature class
6. the new semester
7. the algebra class
8. the journalism class

9. the final examination   10. the debate contest

7. ⇒ Chart IV.
   1. Jennie was very happy yesterday. She's happy today, too.
   (以下続ける)

8. ⇒ Chart IV. (we / she / I の順番に言い換えなさい)
   1. we / We were very happy yesterday. We aren't happy today.
       she / She was very happy yesterday. She isn't happy today.
       I / I was very happy yesterday. I'm not happy today.
   (以下続ける)

9. 例にならい，次の文を否定文にしなさい．
   例) This is an expensive pen. / This isn't an expensive pen.
       They're your brothers. / They're not your brothers.
   1. My name's Bill.
   2. That's my address.
   3. This hotel's very nice.
   4. My room's near the university.
   5. Professor McCarthy's home's on Green Street.
   6. Professor McCarthy's at home now.
   7. The movie's very exciting.
   8. This is a registration card.
   9. That's his wife.
   10. It's very hot today.

10. 例にならい，問題9の各文を疑問文にして，否定で答えなさい．
   例) This is an expensive pen. / Is this an expensive pen? /

No, it isn't.
They're your brothers. / Are they your brothers? / No, they're not.

11. 例にならい，問題9の各文を否定疑問文にして，否定で答えなさい．
例) This is an expensive pen. / Isn't this an expensive pen? / No, it isn't.

12. ⇒ Chart IV.
1. Isn't Jennie happy today? / Yes, she is.
（以下続ける）

13. ⇒ Chart IV.
1. Wasn't Jennie happy yesterday? / No, she wasn't.
（以下続ける）

14. ⇒ Chart III.
1. Aren't you Bill? / Yes, I am.
2. Aren't you Sachiko? / No, I'm not.
（以下続ける）

15. 例にならい，学習者どうしがおたがいに名前を尋ね合う練習をしなさい．
例) —Aren't you Tomiko Nakagawa?
—No, I'm not. I'm Shizuko Fuji.

—Aren't you Takeo Suzuki?
—No, I'm not. I'm Ichiro Kuge.

16. 例にならい，次の語句を使って会話練習をしなさい．

例） —Who's that?
　　—That's Professor McCarthy.
　　—What does he do?
　　—He's an English teacher.
　　—Do you know his wife?
　　—Yes, I do.
　　—What does she do?
　　—She's a music teacher.

　　—Who's that?
　　—That's Mr. Grey.
　　—What does he do?
　　—He's a police officer.
　　—Do you know his wife?
　　—Yes, I do.
　　—What does she do?
　　—She's a pilot.

1. Mr. Jones / a doctor
2. Mr. Shimizu / a dentist
3. Mr. Yamamoto / an artist
4. Mr. Black / a lawyer
5. Mr. Hosokawa / a musician
6. Mr. Brown / a teacher
7. Mr. Shimada / a tailor
8. Mr. Crane / a businessman
9. Mr. Nakamura / a writer

10. Mr. Kent / an exporter

17. 例にならい，問題 16 の語句を使って会話練習をしなさい．
 例) —Who's that?
  —That's Professor McCarthy.
  —Isn't he an English teacher?
  —Yes, he is.

  —Who's that?
  —That's Mr. Grey.
  —Isn't he a police officer?
  —Yes, he is.

18. 例にならい，問題 16 の人名を使って会話練習をしなさい．
 例) —Isn't that Professor McCarthy?
  —Yes, it is. Is he one of your friends?
  —No. But I know his son.

  —Isn't that Mr. Grey?
  —Yes, it is. Is he one of your friends?
  —No. But I know his daughter.

19. 例にならい，前問と同じように会話練習をしなさい．
 例) —Do you know Professor McCarthy?
  —Yes. He and his wife are very interesting people. Would you like to meet them?
  —Yes, I would.

Lesson Five

20. 例にならい，次の語句を使って会話練習をしなさい．
例) —Let me introduce myself. My name is Takeo Ichiyama.
—How do you do? I'm glad to meet you. Aren't you a student here?
—Yes, I am. Aren't you a student, too?
—No, I'm not. I'm a teacher.

1. a doctor
2. an artist
3. a blue-collar worker
4. a professor
5. a scientist
6. a writer
7. a nurse
8. a director
9. a producer
10. a designer

21. ⇒ Chart I.
1. Bob and Dick are playing baseball now.
2. Harry's working at the bookstore now.
（以下続ける）

22. ⇒ Chart I.
1. Are Bob and Dick busy now? / Yes, they are. / What're they doing? / They're playing baseball.
2. Is Harry busy now? / Yes, he is. / What's he doing? / He's working at the bookstore.
（以下続ける）

23. ⇒ Chart IV.
1. What's Jennie doing now? / She's singing.
2. What's Jimmy doing now? / He's crying.
3. taking a nap

4. eating ice cream
5. playing the piano
6. taking a picture
7. drinking beer
8. sleeping at the desk
9. taking medicine

24. ⇒ Chart IV.
1. I saw Jennie yesterday. / Oh? What was she doing? / She was singing.

（以下続ける）

25. ⇒ Chart III.
1. Where's Bill going now? / He's going to Oshima.
2. Where's Sachiko going now? / She's going to the zoo.
3. Who's Peggy calling now? / She's calling Ann.

（以下続ける）

26. 例にならい，名前と住所の会話練習をしなさい．
例）—What's your name?
　　—My name's Takashi Tamada.
　　—What's your address?
　　—39, 3-chome, Kami-machi. I'm living there with my parents now. But I want to find a room near the university.

27. 例にならい，次の語句を使って言い換えなさい．
例）I want to find a room near the university. (office) / I want to find a room near the office. (park) / I want to find a room near

the park.

1. in a hotel
2. near the school
3. in a private home
4. on Green Street
5. on First Avenue
6. in Shinjuku
7. near the Ginza
8. in Naka-ku
9. near the station
10. near the sea

28. 例にならい，次の語句を使って会話練習をしなさい．

例) —I know a nice room on Green Street.
—Is it in a hotel or something?
—No, it isn't. It's in Professor McCarthy's home.
—Isn't he an English professor?
—Yes, he is. Were you one of his students?
—Yes, I was.

—I know a nice room near the university.
—Is it in a hotel or something?
—No, it isn't. It's in Mr. Grey's home.
—Isn't he a police officer?
—Yes, he is. Are you one of his friends?
—Yes, I am.

1. near the park / Mr. Jones / a doctor
2. in the countryside / Mr. Shimizu / a dentist
3. in the city / Mr. Yamamoto / an artist
4. near my office / Mr. Black / a lawyer
5. near the river / Mr. Hosokawa / a musician
6. on Second Street / Mr. Brown / a teacher

7. in Shinjuku / Mr. Shimada / a tailor
8. in Meguro / Mr. Crane / a businessman
9. near the Tokyo Tower / Mr. Nakamura / a writer
10. near the Isemaru Department Store / Mr. Kent / an exporter

29. ⇒ Chart IV.
1. I saw someone last night. / Oh? Who did you see? / I saw a happy girl. / What was she doing? / She was singing.

（以下続ける）

30. ⇒ Chart IV.
1. What did you see? / I saw a girl singing. Did you see a girl singing, too? / No. I didn't see a girl singing. I saw a boy crying.

（以下続ける）

31. ⇒ Chart IV.
1. Which girl is Jennie? / The girl near the window is Jennie.
2. Which boy is Jimmy? / The boy under the table is Jimmy.
3. on the sofa
4. with the ice cream
5. at the piano
6. with the camera
7. with the juice
8. at the desk
9. with the medicine

32. ⇒ Chart IV.
1. Did you see a girl near the window? / Yes, I did. / Was she singing? / Yes, she was.

（問題 31 の語句を使って続ける）

33. ⇒ Chart I.
1. Did you meet some boys in the park? / Yes, I did. / What were they doing? / They were playing baseball.

(以下続ける)

34. 次の話を読み，問いに答えなさい．

This is Bill Cleveland. 'Bill' is short for 'William.' Bill is a student at this school. He was a student here last semester, too. He wants to register for the fall classes. He's talking to the receptionist now. He has to fill in a new registration card. They need a new card every semester. Bill's address is 1964 Superior Avenue. He's living there with his parents now. He doesn't want to stay there. He wants to move. He wants to find a room near the university. The receptionist knows a nice room on Green Street. It's not expensive. It's very cheap. It's not in a hotel. It's in Professor McCarthy's home. Professor McCarthy's an English teacher. Bill was one of his students last year. Bill doesn't know Professor McCarthy's wife. The receptionist knows her very well. Mrs. McCarthy teaches music. She teaches piano and voice. Bill wants to meet her. He wants to see the room, too. The receptionist gave him their address. Bill thanked her for her advice.

1. Who's William Cleveland?
2. What's short for 'William?'
3. Is he a new student?
4. What does he want to do now?
5. Who's he talking to now?
6. What does he have to fill in?

7. Why?
8. What's his address?
9. Is he living alone? Explain.
10. Where does he want to move?
11. Does the receptionist know a room?
12. Is it in a hotel or something?
13. Who's Professor McCarthy?
14. Does Bill know him?
15. Why?
16. Does he know his wife?
17. Isn't Mrs. McCarthy a teacher, too?
18. What does she teach?
19. Where's Professor McCarthy's house?
20. How did Bill get Professor McCarthy's address?

35. 次の問いに答えなさい.
1. What's your address?
2. What's your phone number?
3. Do you live near the school?
4. Do you want to move?
5. Were you a student here last semester?
6. When did you register for this semester?
7. What did you have to do?
8. Did you have to fill out anything? What?
9. Who's your English teacher?
10. Where is his office?

36. 下線の部分に適切な語句を入れなさい.

A: When will you _____ back to school?
B: I'll go _____ in the winter semester.

A: Do you have an apartment _____ the campus?
B: No. I'm staying _____ my uncle's home.

A: Will you _____ a sports team at the university?
B: Yes. I _____ I can join the swim team or something.

A: How _____ do you practice swimming?
B: I practice swimming _____ day.

Lesson Six

A LOOK INTO THE FUTURE
将来の見通し

Section I PRESENTATION CD2-1

Two friends try to make plans to do something together, this afternoon. Their schedules don't match. They can't meet. In Japan, if you tell your friend that you're busy, he says "OK." In the States if you tell your friend that you're busy, he might ask you "Why?"

友人2人が今日の午後いっしょに何かしようと計画をたてようとします。しかし2人の予定が合いません。会うわけにもいきません。日本では'忙しい'と相手に言うと、相手は「はいわかりました」と言います。アメリカでは「忙しい」ということを相手に伝えると、相手は「なぜ?」と聞き返すかもしれません。

Section II APPLICATION DIALOGUE CD2-2

Listen and repeat

A Let's go swimming this afternoon.
B No. Not today. I'm too tired.
A Shall we go to a movie,[1] then?
B I'm sorry, but I'm going to be busy this afternoon.
A Oh? What are you going to do?
B I'm going to see Dr. James.[2] He's going to examine me.
A Don't you feel well?
B Well, I feel tired all the time.
A Do you take vitamins?
B No. I don't need vitamins.
A Yes, you do. I'll go down to the drugstore now. I'll buy you some vitamin pills.
B Let's wait till later. I want to see Dr. James first. I'll ask him about taking vitamins.
A All right. Well, I'm going to go downtown now. I'll be back around six o' clock.
B What are you going to do?

今日の午後泳ぎに行きましょう．
いいえ，今日はダメ．とても疲れているんです．
じゃ，映画に行きましょうか．
残念ですけど，今日の午後はひまになりそうもないんです．
そう？ 何をするんですか．
ジェイムズ先生に診察していただくことになっているんです．
気分がよくないのですか．
そう，このところずっと疲れ気味なんですよ．
ビタミンをとっていますか．
いいえ，ビタミンはいりません．
いや，いりますよ．これから薬局へ行って何かビタミン剤を買ってきてあげましょう．
もう少し待ってみましょう．まずジェイムズ先生に診察してもらって，ビタミンを飲むのがよいかどうか，うかがってみます．
わかりました．ところで，これから街へ行ってきます．6時ごろには戻ってきますからね．
何の用事ですか．

---

1) **go to a movie** 映画を見に行く（go to the movies とも言う）． 2) **see a doctor** 医者にみてもらう．

A I'm going to look around the department store. Maybe I'll buy a few new clothes.

B Well, don't spend all your money.

A Don't worry. I won't.

B Will you get me a copy of *Time* magazine?

A Sure. I'll be glad to. Anything else?

B No. That's all.

A O.K. Well, I'll see you later.

B All right. And take care.

| デパートをのぞいてこようと思います．着るものを少し買うかもしれません． |
| それじゃ，すっからかんにならないようにね． |
| ご心配なく．そんなことはしません． |
| 雑誌の『タイム』を1冊買ってきてくれませんか． |
| いいですとも．お安いご用です．ほかに何か． |
| いや，それだけです． |
| そう．じゃ，またあとで． |
| ええ，気をつけてね． |

Section III NOTES ON CONVERSATIONAL STYLE

1. Let's + 動詞の原形は，人を誘う場合の言い方です．次の例で，答え方もおぼえてください．

    a. *Let's go* downtown. — All right. *Let's do* that.
       （商店街へ行きましょう——わかりました．そうしましょう）

    b. *Let's play* tennis this afternoon. — All right. *Let's do* that.

    c. *Let's buy* some vitamin pills. — No. *Let's not do* that.
       （ビタミン剤を買いましょう——いいえ，やめましょう）

    d. *Let's not go* to Yokohama. — All right. *Let's not go.*

2. Shall we ～? は Let's ～. と同じ意味を表わすことがあります．

    a. *Shall we* go downtown? — Yes. Let's do that.

    b. *Shall we* play tennis this afternoon? — All right. Let's do that.

c. *Shall we* buy some vitamin pills? — No. Let's not do that.
d. *Shall we* go to Yokohama? — No. Let's not go.

Shall I ～? は「(私が)～しましょうか」という相手の気持ちをくんだ申し出を表わします.

Shall I open the window? — Yes, please.
（窓を開けましょうか――ええ，お願いします）

3. Will you ～? は日本語の「～してくれませんか/～してくれない？」に相当します.

a. *Will you* get me a copy of *Time* magazine? — Yes. I'll be glad to.
（タイム誌 1 部買ってきてくれないかな――はい，お安いご用です）
b. *Will you* please close the door? — Sure.
（ドアを閉めてもらえますか――はい，わかりました）
c. *Will you* speak louder? — Yes, I'll be glad to.
（もっと大きな声で話してくれない？――はい，わかりました）

4. be going to + 動詞の原形　しばしばあらかじめ決められた確定している予定の未来の動作・状態を表わします.

a. What *are* you *going to* do tomorrow? — I'*m going to* go downtown.
（明日は何をしますか――街へ行くつもりです）
b. *Are* you *going to* study this afternoon? — No, I'm not. I'*m going to* play *shogi*.
（午後勉強しますか――いいえ，しません．将棋をするつもりです）

c. *Is* he *going to* go to Oshima? — Yes. He'*s going to* go next Tuesday.

　　d. We *are going to* be married next week.（来週結婚の運びです）

▎**5. will** はしばしばはっきりしない（単純）未来の動作・状態を表わすことがあります．

　　a. What are you going to do tomorrow? — I'm not sure. Perhaps I'*ll* go to the movies.

　　b. Is Bill going to go to Oshima? — I don't know. Perhaps he'*ll* go.

　　c. Are they going to study French? — I'm not sure. Perhaps they *won't* study French. Perhaps they'*ll* study German.

▎**6. will** はしばしば日本語の「～してあげます，～してくれる，～してもらう」に相当する気持ちを表わすこともあります．

　　a. I'*ll* help you with your homework. — Thanks a lot.
　　　（宿題を手伝ってあげますよ――たいへんありがとうございます）

　　b. He'*ll* get you some vitamin pills. — That'd be fine.
　　　（彼がビタミン剤を買ってきてくれます――それはありがたい）

　　c. I'*ll* go to the drugstore now. — O.K. Please get me some medicine.
　　　（薬局に行ってあげますよ――わかりました．薬を買ってきてください）

Section IV PRONUNCIATION DRILL CD2-3

▎**1. Pronunciation of *will* and *won't*** （**will** と **won't** の発音）　will はふつう短縮して [l] と発音します．won't (= will not) は [wount] と発音します．

Lesson Six

Listen and repeat

I'll [ail]   you'll [ju:l]   he'll [hi:l]   she'll [ʃi:l]
we'll [wi:l]   they'll [ðeil]   I won't [ai wount]
he won't [hi: wount]   you won't [ju: wount]
I'll go to the store. [ail gòu tə ðə stɔ́r]
He'll play tennis tomorrow. [hi:l plei ténis təmɑrə]
I won't go to school. [ai wòunt gou tə skú:l]

2. Pronunciation of *going to* and *want to*（**going to** と **want to** の発音） going to は短縮して [gɔ́(:)nə/gənə] と言うことがあります．want to は短縮して [wánə] と言うことがあります．

Listen and repeat

I'm going to buy a book. [aim gɔ̀(:)nə bai ə búk]
He's going to play tennis. [hi:z gɔ̀(:)nə plei ténis]
We're going to study hard. [wir gɔ̀(:)nə stʌdi hárd]
We want to go swimming. [wi: wànə gou swímiŋ]
Do you want to play tennis? [du: jə wànə plei ténis]
I don't want to go with you. [ai dount wànə gou wíð ju:]

3. Short forms of *her, his, your, our* （**her, his, your, our** の短縮形）
普通，会話では，こうした語を弱形（weak form）で言います．弱形に対して，はっきり強く言う形を強形（strong form）と呼びます．

Listen and repeat

	Strong form	Weak form
her	[hɚ]	[ɚ]
his	[hiz]	[iz]
your	[ju:r]	[jɚ]

99

our   [aur]   [ar]

Exercise: 次の文を聞いて，例に示してあるような形式で答えなさい．この練習はこうした語が聞きわけられるように耳を馴らすためのものです．

例）*Instructor*　　　　　*Student*
　　Is it his book?　　　Yes, it's Johns.
　　Is it her book?　　　Yes, it's Mary's.
　　Is it your book?　　 Yes, it's mine.
　　Is it our book?　　　Yes, it's ours.

聞き取ってください．音声には次の文が完全な形で入っています．

1. Were they _____ pens?
2. Is it _____ equipment?
3. Are these _____ books?
4. Is it _____ pencil?
5. Was that _____ car?
6. Is it _____ hat?
7. Is it _____ dog?
8. Were they _____ desks?
9. Was it _____ house?
10. Is it _____ paper?

4. Pronunciation of [ou]（[ou] の発音）　[ou] は [o] から始まって，ゆっくりあごを閉じ，[u] で終わります．[o] と [u] の，2 つの母音があるので，二重母音と呼ばれることがあります．まず [o o o o u u u u] 次に [o u o u o u ou ou ou] のように言ってみてください．[ou] と [ɑ] を混同しないでください．

Listen and repeat

1. note [nout]　　not [nɑt]
2. won't [wount]　want [wɑnt]
3. coke [kouk]　　cock [kɑk]
4. boned [bound]　bond [bɑnd]
5. dole [doul]　　doll [dɑl]
6. I won't take any notes. [ai wóunt teik eni nóuts]
7. I want to take some notes. [ai wànə teik səm nóuts]
8. I won't ride on the boat. [ai wóunt raid ɑn ðe bóut]
9. I want to ride on the boat. [ai wànə raid ɑn ðə bóut]

5. Stress　英語のリズムは語勢の強い音節と弱い音節から成りたっています．日本語ですと，文の最後の部分を，しばしば語勢を落として言います．つまり語勢をやわらげ，時としてはほとんど聞こえないくらいのことがあります．英語では，こんなことのないように注意してください．必ず文の最後まで語勢と音量を失わないように心がけてください．語勢のある音節は，語勢のない音節より大きい声で発音しましょう．

Listen and repeat

1. This is the ánswer to my práyer.
   [də də də dá də də də dá]
2. I've been hóping to méet you.
   [də də dá də də dá də]
3. Give me some cáke and a cup of cóffee.
   [də də də dá də də də də dá də]

Answers:　1. her; 2. our; 3. your; 4. his; 5. her; 6. your; 7. his; 8. our;
　　　　　9. her; 10. your.　　　　　　　　　　　　　　(p. 100)

4. He didn't téll me his náme or addréss.
   [də də də dá də də dá də də dá]
5. I tóld him to give me a bóok.
   [de dá də də də də də dá]
6. Gíve the stúdent a pén and some ínk.
   [dá də dá də də dá də də dá]
7. Will you pléase repeat that last wórd?
   [də də dá də də də də dá]
8. Dón't be so impátient.
   [dá də də də dá də]

Section V PATTERN USAGE DRILL CD2-4

Listen and repeat

1. ⇒ Chart I.
   1. Let's play baseball this afternoon. / All right. Let's do that.
   2. Let's go to the bookstore this afternoon. / All right. Let's do that.
   3. Let's go to school this afternoon. / All right. Let's do that.
   （以下続ける）

2. ⇒ Chart III.
   1. Let's go to Oshima. / No. Let's not.
   （以下続ける）

3. 例にならい，Let's と次の語句を使って相手を誘ってみなさい。
   例）play baseball / Let's play baseball. / All right. Let's do that.
   1. play *shogi*　　　　　2. go to a movie

3. go down to the drugstore
4. wait till next week
5. have dinner now
6. go downtown later
7. buy a copy of *Time* magazine
8. look around the department store
9. buy some new clothes
10. buy some vitamin pills

4. 例にならい，Let's not と問題 3 の語句を使って練習しなさい.
例) play baseball / Let's not play baseball. / All right. Let's not.

5. ⇒ Chart I.
1. Shall we play baseball? / Yes. Let's do that.
2. Shall we go to the bookstore? / Yes. Let's do that.
(以下続ける)

6. ⇒ Chart III.
1. Shall we go to Oshima? / Yes. Let's do that. How shall we go? / Let's go by boat. / O.K.
(以下続ける)

7. ⇒ Chart II.
1. Shall we buy a pen and some paper? / No. Let's not buy a pen. Let's just buy some paper. / O.K. Let's do that.
2. get
3. order
4. buy
5. eat
6. ask for
7. sell
8. get
9. ask for

8. ⇒ Chart I.
1. Shall we play baseball this afternoon? / Yes, let's. Where shall we play? / Let's play in the park. / O.K. Let's do that.
2. work
3. study

4. see a Western
5. go swimming
6. work
7. go shopping
8. play tennis
9. go skating

9. 例にならい，問題 3 の語句を使って Shall we 〜? の問いと肯定の答を言いなさい．

例) play baseball / Shall we play baseball? / Yes. Let's do that.

10. 例にならい，問題 9 の問いに断わりの返事をし，理由も言いなさい．

例) Shall we play baseball? / No. Let's not. I don't like baseball. (I have to study. / I have to go downtown this afternoon.)

11. 例にならい，次の語句を使って Shall I 〜? の相手の気持ちをくんだ申し出と肯定の答を言いなさい．

例) get you a magazine / Shall I get you a magazine? / Yes, thanks.

1. ask Dr. James
2. teach you chess
3. buy you some coffee
4. get you a copy of *National Geographic* magazine
5. get you some fruit
6. help you with your studies
7. show you some nice ties
8. show you some new CDs
9. introduce you to Dr. James
10. show you my photo albums

12. 例にならい，問題 11 の Shall I 〜 を使った相手の気持ちをくんだ申し出に断わりの返事をし，その理由も言いなさい．

例) get you a magazine / Shall I get you a magazine? / No, thanks. I don't want to read.

13. 例にならい，問題 11 の語句を使って，I'll ～ の相手の気持ちをくんだ申し出による応答をしなさい．

例) I'll get you a magazine. / Thanks a lot.

14. 例にならい，問題 13 の相手の気持ちをくんだ申し出に断わりの返事をし，その理由を言いなさい．

例) I'll get you a magazine. / No, thanks. I don't want to read.

15. 例にならい，問題 11 の語句を使って Will you～?（人に何かを頼む）で対話をしなさい．

例) Will you get me a magazine? / Sure. I'll be glad to. / Thanks a lot.

16. ⇒ Chart III.
1. Shall we go to Oshima by boat? / No. Let's not go by boat. / Then, how shall we go? / Let's go by plane.
2. Shall we go to the zoo by bus? / No. Let's not go by bus. / Then, how shall we go? / Let's go by car.
3. visit her
4. see it at the theater
5. walk
6. go by car
7. go by boat
8. go by car
9. go on foot

17. ⇒ Chart I.
1. I'm going to play baseball tomorrow. What are you going to do? / Perhaps I'll play baseball, too.

（以下続ける）

18. ⇒ Chart III.
   1. Bill's going to go to Oshima next week. / Oh? How's he going to go? / Perhaps he'll go by boat.

   (以下続ける)

19. ⇒ Chart I.
   1. Are you going to play baseball tomorrow? / No, I'm not. Perhaps I'll go to the bookstore.

   (以下続ける)

20. ⇒ Chart III.
   1. Is Bill going to go to Oshima next week? / I don't know. Perhaps he will.

   (以下続ける)

21. 例にならい，次の語句を使って問いと答を言いなさい．
   例) play tennis / Are you going to play tennis tomorrow? / Yes, I am.
   1. buy some vitamin pills
   2. see Dr. James
   3. buy a copy of *Time* magazine
   4. order some fried eggs
   5. be at home
   6. go downtown
   7. buy some new clothes
   8. go down to the grocery store
   9. stay in a hotel or something
   10. register for the English class

22. 例にならい，問題 21 の問いに否定の返事をしなさい．

例) play tennis / Are you going to play tennis today? / No. I'm not going to play today. Perhaps I'll play tomorrow.

23. 例にならい，問題 21 の語句を使って対話をしなさい．

例) play tennis / I'm going to play tennis. / Oh? When are you going to play? / Perhaps I'll play tomorrow afternoon.

24. 例にならい，問題 21 の語句を使って問いと答を言いなさい．

例) play tennis / Are you going to play tennis today? / Well, perhaps I won't play today. But I'm going to play tomorrow.

25. ⇒ Chart III. 問題 16 の語句を使って対話しなさい．

1. Bill's going to go to Oshima. / Oh? Is he going to go by boat? / Well, perhaps he won't go by boat. Perhaps he'll go by plane.

（以下続ける）

26. ⇒ Chart I.

1. every day / Bob plays baseball every day.
now / Bob's playing baseball now.
yesterday / Bob played baseball yesterday.
tomorrow / Bob's going to play baseball tomorrow.
perhaps—tomorrow / Perhaps Bob'll play baseball tomorrow.

27. ⇒ Chart I.

1. every day / Bob doesn't play baseball every day.
now / Bob isn't playing baseball now.
yesterday / Bob didn't play baseball yesterday.
tomorrow / Bob isn't going to play baseball tomorrow.

perhaps—tomorrow / Perhaps Bob won't play baseball tomorrow.

（以下続ける）

28. 例にならい，次の語句を使って会話練習をしなさい．

例）　—Let's go swimming today.
　　　—No, not today. I'm too tired.
　　　—Shall we go to a movie, then?
　　　—I'm sorry, but I'm going to be busy.

1. play *shogi* / watch television
2. go hiking / have lunch together
3. study German / go to a movie
4. go to the lake / go downtown
5. go shopping / wait till tomorrow
6. visit Harry / wait till this evening
7. go on a picnic / go downtown
8. go down to the drugstore / listen to the radio
9. practice English / read
10. have dinner downtown / go to a play tonight

29. 下線の部分に適切な語句を入れなさい．

A: Are you going to _____ the doctor?
B: No. I'm not going _____ to the doctor.

A: Will you take _____ vitamins?
B: No. I'm not going to take _____ vitamins.

A: What are you going to _____ ?

B: I think I will go to bed and _____ .

A: Are you going to go _____ now?
B: I _____ going home later.

Lesson Seven

HOW HAVE YOU BEEN?
どうしていましたか

Section I PRESENTATION CD2-5

Two friends meet. One friend has been to South America. The other friend has been busy with school. They talk about their other friends. They exchange e-mail addresses. In the States, we don't send New Year cards (*nengajo*), but we send Christmas cards.

2人の友人が会います。1人は南アメリカに行ってきました。もう1人は(学校の)勉強で忙しくしています。2人は自分たち以外の友人のことについて話し合います。Eメールアドレスを交換します。アメリカでは年賀状は送りませんが、クリスマスカードを出します。

Lesson Seven

Section II APPLICATION DIALOGUE CD2-6

Listen and repeat

A Hello. I haven't seen you for a long time. How have you been?
やあ、しばらくでしたね。どうしていましたか？

B I've been fine, thanks. How have you been?
ありがとうございます。元気でしたよ。あなたはどうしていらっしゃいました？

A Well, I've been pretty busy this month. I've been writing a book.
それが、今月はなかなか忙しくてね。本を書いていたものですから。

B That sounds interesting. What kind of book have you been writing?
それはおもしろそうですね。どんな本を書いていらっしゃったのですか。

A A book about my trip to South America.
私の南米旅行記なんです。

B I've always wanted to go to South America. Who went with you?
私はかねがね南米へ行ってみたいと思っていました。だれといっしょでしたか。

A George did. Have you seen him lately?
ジョージといっしょでした。最近彼に会いましたか。

B No, I haven't seen him for a year or so. Is he still a bachelor?
いいえ、かれこれ1年ほど会っていません。彼はまだ独身ですか。

A No. He got married last December.
いや、昨年の12月に結婚しました。

B Married already! How time flies![1] We're all getting old.
もう結婚しましたか。月日のたつのは早いものですね。私たちも、だんだん年をとっていくわけですねえ。

A Yes. I suppose so. You look rather tired today.
まったくですねえ。今日は少し疲れているようですね。

---

1) **How time flies!** 時が早くたつのを飛んでいく矢にたとえて time flies という。

B I've been studying all night. I still go to school, you know. I'm having an exam tomorrow.

A Well, good luck.[1]

B Thanks. I'll need it.[2] By the way, Where's George now? I'd like to see him again.

A He's gone to Chicago. I've been there myself, you know. That's why I haven't seen you lately.

B Are you going back soon?

A Yes. I'm leaving tomorrow.

B That's too bad. I want to talk to you more.

A Well, here's my e-mail address. Please keep in touch.

B Thank you. I'll be sure to send you an e-mail Christmas card.

A I must go now. Hope to see you again soon.

B Me, too. Bye for now.

昨晩，徹夜で勉強していたものですから．私はまだ学校へ行っておりますのでね．明日試験なんですよ．

それはそれは！ 首尾よくやってください．

ありがとうございます．そうありたいものですがね．ところでジョージは今どちらに？ もう一度会いたいものです．

シカゴに行ってますよ．私もずっとあちらなんです．ですからこのところあなたに会わなかったわけなんです．

近くお帰りになるのですか．

ええ，明日発ちます．

それは残念です．もっとお話したかったのですが．

えっと，私のメールアドレスです．どうぞご連絡ください．

ありがとうございます．必ずメールでクリスマスカードをお送りします．

さあ行かなければなりません．またすぐお会いできますよ．

私もそう思いますよ．ではさようなら．

---

1) **good luck**「試験がうまくゆくように祈る」の意味．

2) **I'll need it.** の it は，相手の言った good luck をさし，「運に恵まれて試験がうまくゆけばいいが」の意味．

Section III NOTES ON CONVERSATIONAL STYLE

1. 現在形と現在完了形の違い

a. 今英語を勉強しています．
b. この3年間英語を勉強しています．

英語では上記の a. の意味を表わすのに，Lesson 5 で習った 'be + ～ing' を使います．b. の意味を表わすのには 'have + 過去分詞' の型(現在完了形)を使います．次の例文を比べて意味の違いを確かめてください．

a. I *am studying* English now.
（私は今英語を勉強しています）
I *have studied* English for three years.
（私はこの3年間英語を勉強しています）

b. I *am living* in Tokyo now.
（私は今東京に住んでいます）
I *have lived* in Tokyo for ten years.
（私は東京にこの10年ずっと住んでいます）

c. He *is* sick now.
（今彼は病気です）
He *has been* sick since last Sunday.
（彼はこの前の日曜日からずっと病気です）

2. 過去形と現在完了形の違い
動詞の過去形は過去の特定の時の動作・状態を表わします．'have + 過去分詞' は過去のある時から現在までの間の動作・状態を表わします．

a. I *came* here three years ago. 〈過去の特定の時〉
I *have lived* here for three years. 〈現在までの期間〉

  b. I *knew* him in 2001.〈過去の特定の時〉
   I'*ve known* him since 2001.〈現在までの期間〉
  c. I *didn't see* you last month.〈過去の特定の時〉
   I *haven't seen* you for a month.〈現在までの期間〉

 次の日本文を比べてください．

  a. 彼女は昨日ケーキを作りました．
  b. 彼女はちょうどケーキを作ったところです．

 英語では上記の a. の意味を表わすのには過去形を用います．b. の意味を表わすためには 'have + 過去分詞' を用います．次の例文を比べて意味の違いを確かめてください．

  a. She *made* a cake yesterday.
   （彼女は昨日ケーキを作りました）
   She *has* just *made* a cake.
   （彼女はちょうどケーキを作ったところです）
  b. He *bought* a book last week.
   （彼は先週本を買いました）
   He *has* just *bought* a book.
   （彼はちょうど本を買ったところです）

3. 現在完了形は動作の性質によって完了形の意味が変りますので注意が必要です．
 a.「話す，歩く，学ぶ」など終わりがはっきりしない動詞を完了形に使うとこれまでの実績をまとめて表現することになりますが，動作が最終的に完結したことにはなりません．

  1) I *have studied* English for three years.
   〈今日までの英語学習暦が 3 年ある〉

2）I *have read* the five chapters.
（5 章まで読み終えました）
3）We *have* already *flown* for 12 hours.
（離陸してから 12 時間になります）
4）I *haven't seen* you for a long time.
（長く会っていません）

b. 動詞が状態の意味を表わす場合は完了形でも完了の意味を持ちません．

1）I *have lived* in Tokyo all my life.
〈生まれてから他の場所には住んだことがない〉
2）I *have been* down with a bad cold for the past two weeks.
（ひどい風邪で 2 週間寝込んでいます）
3）I *have been* fine, thanks.
（ずっと元気でしたよ）

c. すでに済んでしまった状態に対しても現在完了形が使われることがあります．

a）Somebody *has been* in our garden.
（誰かがうちの庭に入った形跡があります）
b）Where *have* you *been* all this time?
（いままでどこにいたんですか）
c）I *have been* to London.
（ロンドンから帰ったところです）〈この意味では前置詞に to を用います〉

「到着する，出発する，会う，持って来る，ぶつかる，落ちる；始まる，終わる」など動作の終結が含まれていると，完了形はその動作がつい最近終わりを遂げた意味となります．「部分的な完了」とは異なることに注意してください．

Our plane *has* already *landed*.〈着陸したがまだ乗客は機内にいる〉

　この用法では「ひとつの動作は終わったばかりで次の動作がまだ始まらない，痕跡がまだ生々しい，ほとぼりがまだ覚めやらない」という含みがあります．この点で過去形と区別されます．

The concert ended half an hour ago (the hall is now empty).
（演奏は30分前に終わって，ホールに人の気配はもうない）

　また recently, lately などの副詞を添え，ぼんやりと最近の出来事であることを示唆することもあります．けっこうよく使われる言い方です．語法上誤りだと主張する人もいますが，けっしてそんなことはありません．

Have you *seen* him *lately*?（最近彼に会いましたか）
Only *recently* the negotiation *has started* to make any progress.
Most *recently* my mother *has been suffering* from her broken leg.

4. 現在完了形は次のような語句といっしょに使います．

just, today, this morning [week, year], since last year, since 1980, since childhood, for ten years [three weeks, two hours] など．

5. 状態を表わす動詞（p. 76 の 5. 参照）は 'be＋〜ing 形' では使えませんが 'have＋過去分詞' には用いることができます．

　a. He was very busy last week.（先週は）
　　 He *has been* very busy this week.（今週ずうっと）
　b. I belonged to the YMCA three years ago.（3年前は）
　　 I *have belonged* to the YMCA for three years.（ここ3年ずうっと）

6. 現在完了形の疑問文は，次のように主語と助動詞 have を置き換えて作ります．

　　a. You *have* studied English. → *Have* you studied English?
　　b. He *has* gone to India. → *Has* he gone to India?
　　c. You *have* been to London. → *Have* you been to London?

7.「(今まで)〜へ行ってきた」は，普通 'have been (to 〜)' で表わします．

　　a. I've *been* to London. (ロンドンへ行ってきました)
　　b. Where *have* you *been*? (どこへ行ってきたのですか)

8. 過去に始まり現在まで続いている動作を強調して表わすときには 'have + 過去分詞' でなく **'have been + 〜ing'** の形を用いることがあります．次の例を比較してください．

　　a. I *have studied* English since 1997.
　　　(1997 年から英語を勉強しています)
　　　I *have been studying* English since 1997.
　　　(1997 年から英語を勉強し続けています)
　　b. He *has eaten* the peanuts.
　　　(彼はピーナッツを食べ終わったところです)
　　　He *has been eating* peanuts today.
　　　(彼は今日ピーナッツを食べてばかりいます)

9.「現在完了進行形」は「現在進行形」を基にしていますので，「現在進行形」がなければ「現在完了進行形」もありません．

　　正: I have belonged to the YMCA for three years.
　　誤: I have been belonging to the YMCA for three years.

10. 'be + ～ing' は，未来の確定した予定を表わすことがあります．

a. I'*m going* to Chicago tomorrow.
（明日シカゴへ行きます）
b. I'*m having* an exam next week.
（来週試験があります）

Section IV PRONUNCIATION DRILL CD2-7

1. Short forms of *have* and *has*（have と has の短縮形）

Listen and repeat

	Full form	Short form
I have	[ai hæv]	[aiv]
you have	[juː hæv]	[juːv]
he has	[hiː hæz]	[hiːz]
we have	[wiː hæv]	[wiːv]
they have	[ðei hæv]	[ðeiv]
what have	[wət hæv]	[wət əv]
how have	[hau hæv]	[hau əv]
What have you done?	[wɑ́t hæv juː dʌn]	[wɑ́dəv jə dʌn]

2. Pronunciation of [θ] and [ð]（[θ] と [ð] の発音）　まず舌の先を上下の歯の間に置きます．次に，舌と上歯の間から強く息を出すと，[θ] を発音したことになります．[ð] を発音する場合の舌と歯の位置は [θ] とまったく同じで，ただ有声音にするだけが違います．[θ] と [s]，[ð] と [z] をまちがえないように注意してください．

　[θ, ð] では，必ず舌の先を上下の歯の間におくことが大切なのですが，舌を出し過ぎて，歯と歯の間に完全にはさんでしまうと，別の音になることがあります．次ページの図のように，舌の先が上歯の先に軽く接する程度でよいので

す．一般に，この [ð] という音はあまりしばしば英語には出てこないのですが，そのくせ日常会話で最もよく使われる語の中に出てくるのです．

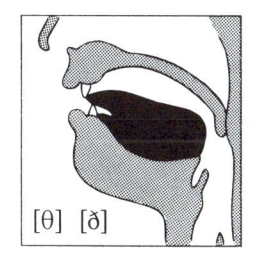

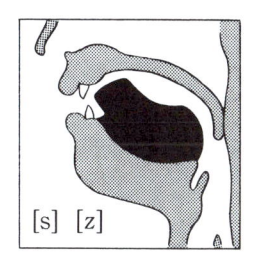

[θ] [ð]　　　　[s] [z]

Listen and repeat

1. theme [θiːm]　　　seem [siːm]
2. thick [θik]　　　sick [sik]
3. thought [θɔt]　　　sought [sɔt]
4. mouth [mauθ]　　　mouse [maus]
5. moth [mɔθ]　　　moss [mɔs]
6. bathe [beið]　　　bays [beiz]
7. breathe [briːð]　　　breeze [briːz]

　　this [ðis]　　　those [ðouz]
　　that [ðæt]　　　than [ðæn]
　　they [ðei]　　　the [ðə]
　　them [ðem]　　　there, their [ðer]
　　these [ðiːz]

3. Double vowels（Diphthongs）（二重母音 [ai] [au] [ɔi] [ei] [ou]）このうち [ei] と [ou] はすでに学びましたが，残りの3つの二重母音の発音はそれほどむずかしくはありません．

Listen and repeat

high [hai]	how [hau]	hoist [hɔist]
my [mai]	mouth [mauθ]	moist [mɔist]
sigh [sai]	sow [sau]	soil [sɔil]

4. Stress exercise 次の英文を聞いてください．それぞれのグループの文が同じリズムをもっていることに注意してください．

Listen and repeat

1. Whát did you dó at the stóre?
   Whý did you téll him to gó?
   Dón't give me ány more téa.
2. Have you séen my bróther?
   Did you síng last níght?
   I can sénd the bóok.
3. Give him an ápple, a péar, and a pén.
   I'll take a bóttle, a bóx, and some stríng.
   We saw a rábbit, a skúnk, and a snáke.

次のグループでは，拍子と拍子の間にいくら余計な音節がきてもリズムに変化のないことに注意してください．

> The bóok was ínteresting.
> The red bóok was ínteresting.
> The red bóok you gave me was ínteresting.
> The red bóok you gave me was very ínteresting.
> The red bóok you gave me last night was very ínteresting.

5. Intonation review 次の文を読みなさい（抑揚パターン 2-3-1 および 2-3 の復習）．

Listen and repeat

aim gouiŋ tə toukiou ai θiŋk juː ʃud kʌm əlɔŋ tuː ðer ɚ meniː intrəstiŋ saits tə siː ænd aim ʃɚ juːd hæv ə gud taim hau əbaut miːtiŋ miː ət siks əklɑk in frʌnt əv ðə steiʃən əd biː fain

həlou iz ðis ði ei biː siː iŋgliʃ skuːl aid laik tə æsk əbaut jɚ klæsiz duː jə hæv eni in ði iːvniŋ frəm siks əklɑk tuː aurz evri nait hau mʌtʃ iz ðe tuːiʃən ɑr ðer eni ʌðɚ ekspensiz ai siː θæŋk ju veri mʌtʃ ail kɔl əgen leitɚ gud bai

> I'm going to Tokyo. I think you should come along too. There are many interesting sights to see. And I'm sure you'd have a good time. How about meeting me at six o'clock? In front of the station would be fine.
>
> Hello. Is this the ABC English School? I'd like to ask about your classes. Do you have any in the evening? From six o'clock? Two hours every night? How much is the tuition? Are there any other expenses? I see. Thank you very much. I'll call again later. Good-bye.

Section V PATTERN USAGE DRILL CD2-8

Listen and repeat

1. ⇒ Chart I.

   1. Did Bob play baseball yesterday? / No, he didn't. / Has he

played today? / Yes, he has.

（以下続ける）

2. ⇒ Chart IV.
1. How's Jennie? / She's been happy all day.

（以下続ける）

3. ⇒ Chart III.
1. Does Bill want to go to Oshima? / Yes. He's wanted to go to Oshima for a long time.

（以下続ける）

4. ⇒ Chart I.
1. Have they played baseball very long? / Yes, they have. They've played baseball for two years.
2. for several years
3. since 2001
4. since his childhood
5. since 1997
6. all summer
7. shopped at that store / for three years
8. for ten years
9. for a long time

5. ⇒ Chart III.
1. Where's Bill? / He's gone to Oshima.
2. Where's Sachiko? / She's gone to the zoo.
3. Where's Peggy? / She's gone to Ann's.

4. Where's Mr. Fox? / He's gone to the soccer match.

(以下続ける)

6. ⇒ Chart III.
   1. Have you seen Bill today? / No. I haven't seen him today. But I saw him yesterday.

(以下続ける)

7. ⇒ Chart I.
   1. Have you played baseball this week? / No. I haven't played baseball this week. But I played last week.

(以下続ける)

8. ⇒ Chart IV.
   1. Does Jennie sing every day? / Yes, she does. But she hasn't sung today.

(以下続ける)

9. ⇒ Chart IV.
   1. Has Jennie sung this afternoon? / No. She hasn't sung this afternoon. But she sang this morning.

(以下続ける)

10. ⇒ Chart I.
   1. Have you been to the park today? / No, I haven't. I've been to the bookstore.
   2. Have you been to the bookstore today? / No, I haven't. I've been to school.

11. ⇒ Chart III.
  1. Bill's gone to Oshima. / No. He hasn't gone to Oshima. He's gone to the zoo.
  2. Sachiko's gone to the zoo. / No. She hasn't gone to the zoo. She's gone to Peggy's.

  （以下続ける）

12. 例にならい，次の文を現在完了形にして言いなさい．
  例) He worked at the store twenty years ago. / He's worked at the store for twenty years.
  You wanted a new car last year. / You've wanted a new car since last year.
  1. They studied English three years ago.
  2. He lived in Mexico three months ago.
  3. You wanted to study English in 2000.
  4. He was in China last December.
  5. She was pretty busy two weeks ago.
  6. They were in Tokyo last Tuesday.
  7. He wanted to go to the United States last spring.
  8. You wanted to go down to the drugstore this morning.
  9. She worked at a department store five years ago.
  10. He was a student here last semester.

13. 例にならい，問題 12 の各文を言い換えなさい．
  例) He worked at that store twenty years ago. / Has he worked at that store for twenty years? / No. He hasn't worked there for twenty years. He's just worked there for fifteen years.
  You wanted a new car last year. / Have you wanted a new car

since last year? / No. I haven't wanted one since last year. I've just wanted one since last month.

14. 例にならい，次の語を使って会話練習をしなさい．
例) —Hello. I haven't seen you for a long time. How have you been?
—Well, I've been pretty busy this month. How have you been?
—I've been pretty busy, too.
1. sick   3. ill   5. fine
2. tired   4. upset

15. ⇒ Chart I.
1. What's Bob doing now? / He's playing baseball. He's been playing all day.
(4, 7 を除いて続ける)

16. ⇒ Chart IV.
1. What's Jennie doing now? / She's singing. She's been singing all afternoon.
(以下続ける)

17. 例にならい，問題 12 の文を現在完了進行形の問いと答に言い換えなさい．
例) He worked at that store twenty years ago. / Has he been working at that store very long? / Yes, he has. He's been working there for twenty years.
You wanted a new car last year. / Have you been wanting[1] a

---

1) 比較的長時間 want (ほしい) の状態が続いている場合，必要があると理解され，現在完了進行形として使われることがあります．

new car very long? / Yes, I have. I've been wanting a new car since last year.

(4, 6, 10 を除いて続ける)

18. 例にならい，次の語句を使って会話練習をしなさい．

例) —I haven't seen you all week. What have you been doing?
　　—I've been writing a book.
1. painting my house
2. studying history
3. staying home
4. camping in the mountains
5. sightseeing in Kyoto
6. working at the hospital
7. staying in Hakone
8. studying for the entrance examination
9. practicing tennis every day
10. hiking in the countryside

19. 例にならい，問題 18 の文を言い換えなさい．

例) —Have you been writing a book?
　　—No, I haven't. I've been painting my house.

20. 例にならい，次の語を使って会話練習をしなさい．

例) —I took a trip to South America.
　　—That sounds interesting. I've always wanted to go to South America. Who went with you?
　　—George did. Have you seen him lately?

—No. I haven't seen him for a year or so.[1]

1. Mexico
2. England
3. Germany
4. France
5. Switzerland
6. China
7. Hawaii
8. Singapore
9. Paris
10. London
11. Korea
12. Brazil

21. 例にならい，問題 20 の各文を言い換えなさい．

例） —Where's your brother?

—He's gone to South America. I've been there, too.

22. 会話練習（学習者は結婚していることを想定して）

例） —Are you married?

—Yes, I am.

—When did you get married?

—I got married last December.

—Who did you marry?

—I married a girl from Akita Prefecture.

23. 会話練習

例） —Where's your home?

—In Nagoya.

—Are you going back soon?

—Yes, I'm leaving next week.

24. ⇒ Chart III.

1. What's Bill doing tomorrow? / He's going to Oshima tomorrow.

（以下続ける）

---

1) **for a year or so** 1 年間かそこら．

25. ⇒ Chart I.
　1. What's Bob doing next Sunday? / He's playing baseball next Sunday.
　2. What's Harry doing next Monday? / He's working at the bookstore next Monday.
（以下続ける）

26. 会話練習
　例）—What are you doing tomorrow?
　　　—Well, I'm playing tennis tomorrow afternoon. What are you doing?
　　　—I'm going to the movies.

27. 下線の部分に適切な語句を入れなさい．
A: ＿＿＿＿＿ have you been?
B: I've been busy ＿＿＿＿＿ school.

A: What have you ＿＿＿＿＿ studying?
B: I've been reading ＿＿＿＿＿ science book.

A: ＿＿＿＿＿ you been reading all day?
B: No, I haven't. I ＿＿＿＿＿ a short nap in the afternoon.

A: Have you been studying ＿＿＿＿＿ our math test tomorrow?
B: Oh. No! I've been studying the ＿＿＿＿＿ subject.

Lesson Eight
GOING TO THE MOVIES
映画を見に行く

Section I PRESENTATION CD2-9

Taro and Jimmy are planning to see a movie. They make plans for when and where to meet. After the movie they will go to Taro's home for a meal and a piece of homemade pie. In the States, it is common to invite friends to one's home for parties and meals. In Japan, homes are often too small to have home parties.

太郎とジミーは映画を見に行く計画を練っています．いつ，どこで会うか計画を立てます．映画を見たら太郎の家に寄って料理と自家製のパイを食べる予定です．米国では自分の家に友人を招いてパーティや食事するのが当り前です．日本では家がせまいので，そのようなことは，まずありません．

Section II APPLICATION DIALOGUE CD2-10

A Wow! Taro! I haven't seen you in a long time. How have you been?

おーい！太郎じゃないか！長いことごぶさただね．どうしていたの

B Hello, Jimmy! I've been fine, but very busy. Nice to see you again.

今日は．ジミー．ずっと元気だよ．でもとても忙しくてね．また会えて何よりだよ．

A If you have some free time this week, we should get together. We have a lot to talk about.

今週時間があるなら，会いたいね．お互いつもる話があるよ．

B I'm sorry, but I'm not free this week. I might have some time next week. How about you, are you free on Saturday, next week?

申し訳ないけど今週は時間ないんだ．来週だったら少し時間できるかもしれないけど．君の方はどう？　来週の土曜日，時間できない？

A Sure, let's meet next week, Saturday. What should we do?

大丈夫だよ．来週，土曜日に（ゆっくり）会おうよ．どうするかな．

B How about coming to my home? I can cook you a meal.

ぼくの家に来たらどうかな．食事作るよ．

A That might be fun. But there is a new film from America. I want to see it. The newspaper's review said you must see it.

それはおもしろいかもしれないね．だけど，新しいアメリカ映画があって，見たいんだよ．新聞の映画評によれば，必見だそうだ．

B O.K. But, that movie might be in Japanese. Can you understand Japanese?

いいね．でもその映画，日本語の吹替えかもしれないね．君，日本語わかる？

A I can't understand Japanese that well. We should go to a movie with subtitles. Then we can both under-

日本語はそんなによくわからないね．字幕付きの映画だったら行ってもいいね．それなら２人とも映画がわかるというものだね．

stand the movie.

B Sounds good. Where should we meet? その方がいいね. どこで会おうかな.

A Let's meet at Baba-cho Station. It has only one ticket gate. Have you ever been there? 馬場町駅で会おうよ. 改札口一つだから. 行ったことある?

B Yes, I have. All right. What time should I be at the train station? あるよ. 了解. 何時に駅で会おうか.

A Well, the movie starts at 1:00 pm, so we should meet at 12:30. えーと. 映画は1時に始まるから, 12時半に落ち合おうよ.

B By the way, what is the movie about? ところで, どんな映画なの.

A It's a remake of a Japanese horror movie. You know that Japanese movies and animation are very popular in America these days. 日本のホラー(恐怖)映画の焼き直しだよ. 日本の映画や動画(アニメ)は, このところアメリカでもずいぶん人気があるだろう.

B It will be interesting to see a Japanese movie, in English. After the movie, you can come to my home and I will cook a dinner for us. And we can have a piece of homemade pie. 日本映画を英語版で見るなんて面白いだろうね. 映画が終わったらぼくの家に寄ってよ. ごちそうこしらえてあげる. 自家製のパイもあるよ.

A That sounds great! Count me in.[1] そりゃあ, すごい. お相伴にあずかるよ.

---

1) **count ~ in** ～を含める, 仲間に入れる.

Section III NOTES ON CONVERSATIONAL STYLE

1. 日本語の「今までに～したことがあります」という「経験」を表わす英語は **'have + 過去分詞'** の型を使います.

 a. I'*ve talked* to her many times.
  （何回も彼女と話したことがあります）
 b. He'*s been* to Hokkaido once.
  （彼は一度北海道へ行ったことがあります）
 c. I'*ve* never *seen* such a beautiful painting.
  （こんな美しい絵を見たことがない）

2. 上記の 1. の疑問文には ever を用いることがありますが，答の文には用いません.

 a. Have you *ever* been to Hokkaido?
  （北海道へ行ったことがありますか）
  Yes, I have. / No, I haven't.
  （ええ，あります. / いいえ，ありません）
 b. Has she *ever* acted in a play?
  （彼女は芝居に出たことがありますか）
  Yes, many times. / No, never.
  （はい，何回も. / いいえ，一度もありません）

3. can（could） は技能，能力，可能性，**might** は可能性，**may** は可能性を表わします．会話における可能性の具体的内容は，頼む・要望する / 同意・容認を求める / 助言・提案する，が中心です．[1] **should** は義務・当然を

---

[1] なお，「許可」と言われる場合は法律・規則などに限られるのが普通で，個人の日常生活では原則ありません．

表わします．～ing や継続形をとりません．語尾変化もありません．疑問文は主語と助動詞を置き換えて作ります．

a. **can, could**（～することができる / できた）
1) He *can* play tennis.
   Can he play tennis? — Yes, he *can*. [No, he *can't*.]
   He *can't* play tennis today.
   Can't he play tennis? — Yes, he *can*. [No, he *can't*.]
   Jane *can* speak German fluently.
   （ドイツ語を流暢に話します）
   Jane *can* go shopping this afternoon.
   （今日の午後なら買物に行けます）
   Can I have a glass of water?
   （水一杯お願いします）
2) I *could* play the piano many years ago.
   I *couldn't* play the piano in 1990.
   Could you play the piano in 1990? — Yes, I *could*.
   Couldn't you play the piano in 1990? — No, I *couldn't*.

b. **may/might**（～かもしれない）〈may と might では，may のほうがあらたまった言いまわし〉
1) I *may/might* go shopping.
   （買物に行くかもしれない）
2) I *may/might* be busy this weekend.
   （私はこの週末は忙しいかもしれない）
3) He *may/might* come to the party.
   （彼はパーティに来るかもしれない）
4) We *may/might* not go to the mountains.

(ぼくたちは山へ行かないかもしれない)

  c. **may/can**（〜してもいいです）——相手の意向，行動に同意したり，容認する。〈may と can では，may のほうがていねいな言いまわし〉
  1) *May/Can* I eat my lunch now? Yes, you *may/can*. [No, you *may/can* not.]
   (今おべんとうを食べてもいいですか。ええ，よろしい。[いいえ，いけません])
  2) You *may/can* go to the movies.
   (映画を見に行ってもいいですよ)
  3) You *may/can* not bring the dog in the house.
   (家の中に犬をつれてきてはだめですよ)
  4) He *may not/cannot* eat any more cake.
   (彼はこれ以上ケーキを食べてはだめです)

  d. **should**（〜すべきだ/〜するのがよい）
  1) You *should* study harder.
   (あなたはもっと勉強しなさいよ)
  2) He *should* study English.
   (彼は英語を勉強したほうがいい)
  3) We *shouldn't* get mad.
   (私たちはおこってはいけない)
  4) You *shouldn't* spend so much money.
   (あなたはそんなにお金を使ってはいけない)
  5) *Should* we go now?
   (今，行くほうがよいでしょうか)

4. 数えられない名詞でも，数えられる分類語を添えれば，間接的に数える

Lesson Eight

ことができます.

    a. I like pottery. I have a few *pieces of* pottery.

piece は furniture, cake, pie, butter, toast, advice, chalk, soap, paper, meat, cloth, candy のようなものの数を表わす場合に使います.

    b. I like milk. I have a *bottle of* milk.

bottle, box, bag は, 容器に入れた液体・粉末・固形物などの数を表わす場合に使います.

    bottle: ink, milk, beer, juice, etc.
    box: candy, sugar, etc.
    bag: flour, salt, etc.

5. you は,「一般的にだれでも」の意味に使うことがあります.

    a. *You* can get to Oshima by plane.（= It is possible to go to Oshima by plane.）
    （大島へは飛行機で行けます）

    b. Can *you* buy Hagi-yaki in Tokyo?（= Is Hagi-yaki sold in Tokyo?）
    （萩焼は東京で買えますか）

Section IV PRONUNCIATION DRILL CD2-11

Pronunciation of final [ts]（語尾 [ts] の発音）　日本語では tsubame, tsume, tsuru などのように, 語のはじめに [ts] が用いられますが, 英語では tsetse [tsétsi]（ツェツェバエ）のようなわずかの外来語を除いては, 語のはじめに [ts] を使うことはありません. [ts] は語尾にくるのがふつうです.

Listen and repeat

▌**1.** [t] で終わる名詞の複数形は [ts] で終わり，[t] で終わる語が is と結びついたときも [ts] となります．

 bat [bæt]   bats [bæts]
 hat [hæt]   hats [hæts]
 it is [it iz]   it's [its]
 that is [ðæt iz] that's [ðæts]

▌**2.** [t] で終わる動詞の現在形は，he, she, it などや単数の名詞（3人称単数）といっしょに用いられると [ts] となります．

 I hit it. [ai hit it] He hits it. [hi: hits it]
 I beat it. [ai bi:t it] She beats it. [ʃi: bí:ts it]

▌**3.** [t] で終わる語の所有格は [ts] となります．

 the cat [ðə kæt] the cat's paw [ðə kæts pɔ:]
 Mat [mæt] Mat's hat [mæts hæt]

Exercise: 次の各語の複数を発音してください．
 cat, rat, hat, mat, seat, pleat, beet, sight, night, right, light

Exercise: 次の各文を短縮形を使って発音してください．
 What is your name?
 That is too bad.
 Pat is here.
 The hat is on the table.
 The meat is too expensive.
 The light is still on.

Lesson Eight

Section V PATTERN USAGE DRILL CD2-12

Listen and repeat

1. ⇒ Chart I.
1. Have you ever played baseball? / Yes, I have.

（以下続ける）

2. ⇒ Chart III.
1. Have you ever been to Oshima? / No, I haven't.
2. been to the zoo
3. met Peggy and Ann
4. met Mr. Fox
5. been to the movies with Haruko
6. been to the mountains with Mike

（以下続ける）

3. 例にならい，次の語句を使って現在完了形の疑問文と答を言いなさい．
例) play chess / Have you ever played chess? / Yes, I have. Have you? / Yes, I have.
1. collected folk pottery
2. been to Mashiko
3. heard of Masihko-yaki
4. heard of Dr. Martin Luther King, Jr.
5. been to Nikko by car
6. seen a Japanese musical
7. been late for an appointment
8. been late for class
9. met Professor McCarthy

10. seen any pieces of folk pottery

4. 例にならい，問題3の語句を使って言い換えなさい．
   例) play chess / Have you ever played chess? / No, I've never played chess. Have you ever played chess? / Yes, I have. I've played chess many times.

5. 例にならい，Have you ever〜? の文を各自で作りなさい．
   例) Have you ever studied German? / No, I haven't.
   Have you ever studied American History? / Yes, I have.

6. 例にならい，次の語句を使って会話練習をしなさい．
   例) —I've been to Hachijo-jima.
   —I've never heard of it. What's it famous for?
   —It's famous for its fine beaches.
   1. Yokohama / its Chinatown
   2. Switzerland / its mountains
   3. France / its fine food
   4. Africa / its animals
   5. Chicago / its tall buildings
   6. Kobe / its port
   7. Cleveland / its universities
   8. the Takarazuka Theater / its musicals
   9. Las Vegas / its gambling
   10. Akihabara / its interesting electrical goods

7. 例にならい，問題6の語句を使って会話練習をしなさい．
   例) —Have you ever been to Hachijo-jima?

Lesson Eight

—No. I've never been there. But I've heard of it.
—What have you heard about it?
—It's famous for its fine beaches.

8. 例にならい，次の語句を使って「経験」を問う疑問文を作り，quite a few または quite a lot を使って答えなさい．

例）Have you ever bought any folk pottery? / Yes. I've bought quite a lot of folk pottery.
Have you ever seen any pieces of folk pottery? / Yes, I've seen quite a few pieces.

1. eaten any sukiyaki
2. seen any Mashiko-yaki
3. bought any pieces of Hagi-yaki
4. played chess
5. studied German
6. studied American History
7. seen any musicals
8. taken vitamin pills
9. read any copies of *Time* magazine
10. studied French

9. 例にならい，次の語句を使って問いと答を言いなさい．

例）folk pottery (pieces) / How much folk pottery do you have? / Oh? I have quite a lot. I have twenty or thirty pieces of folk pottery.

1. furniture (pieces)
2. milk (bottles/cartons)
3. bread (loaves/slices)
4. paper (pieces/sheets)

5. butter (pats/sticks)
6. meat (slices/ounces)
7. soap (bars/pieces)
8. juice (bottles/cans)
9. sugar (bags)
10. pie (pieces/slices)
11. candy (bags/pieces)
12. gum (packages/sticks)
13. flower (bunches)
14. cloth (pieces)
15. jam (jars)
16. toothpaste (tubes)
17. coffee (cans/pounds)

10. 例にならい，問題9の語句を使って言い換えなさい．

例) What would you like? / I'd like a piece of folk pottery.

11. 例にならい，次の語を使って問いと答を言いなさい(問いの部分で数えられる名詞には many，数えられない名詞には much を使うこと)．

例) gum / Do you have many pieces of gum? / Yes. I have seven or eight.

chocolate / Do you have much chocolate? / Yes. I have three or four bars.

1. furniture
2. idea
3. bread
4. fruit
5. English class
6. time
7. work
8. poem
9. poetry
10. novel

12. 例にならい，問題6の語句を使って会話練習をしなさい．

例) —Can you tell me about Hachijo-jima?
　　—Yes, I can. It's famous for its beaches.
　　—Can you go there by plane?
　　—Yes, you can. You can go by boat, too.

13. ⇒ Chart III.
    1. What shall we do tomorrow? / Well, we can go to Oshima. Shall we do that? / O.K. What time can you meet me? / At ten o'clock. / Fine.

    (3, 7 を除いて以下続ける)

14. 例にならい，次の語句を使って会話練習をしなさい．
    例) —Can you play the piano?
    —No, I can't play the piano now. I could play ten or twelve years ago. But I've forgotten now.
    1. play the violin
    2. play chess
    3. skate
    4. say the Greek alphabet
    5. play the mandolin
    6. play soccer
    7. speak French
    8. drive
    9. ski
    10. play the flute

15. ⇒ Chart I.
    1. Can Bob play baseball today? / No. He can't play today. / Oh? Why not? / He's too busy to play.
    2. sick   4. busy   6. sick   8. old
    3. ill   5. tired   7. busy   9. tired

16. ⇒ Chart I.
    1. What're Bob and Dick going to do this afternoon? / I'm not sure. They might play baseball, or they might work at the bookstore.
    2. What's Harry going to do this afternoon? / I'm not sure. He might work at the bookstore, or he might go to school.

（以下続ける）

17. ⇒ Chart III.
  1. What're you going to do tomorrow? / I'm not sure. I might go to Oshima or I might go to the zoo.
  2. What're you going to do tomorrow? / I'm not sure. I might go to the zoo or I might visit Peggy.

（以下続ける）

18. ⇒ Chart II.
  1. What are you going to buy? / I'm not sure. I might buy a pen, or I might buy some paper.
  2. get   4. want   6. need   8. give away
  3. order   5. eat   7. buy   9. ask for

19. ⇒ Chart III.
  1. Bill's going to Oshima next week. / Oh? How's he going to go? / I'm not sure. He might go by boat.
  2. go to the zoo / by bus
  3. talk to Ann / by phone
  4. see the boxing match / on television

（以下続ける）

20. 例にならい，会話練習をしなさい．
  例) What are you going to do tomorrow? / I'm not sure. I might look around the department store, or I might go to a movie.

21. ⇒ Chart III.
  1. May I go to Oshima with you? / Sure. Please come along.

2. May I go to the zoo with you? / Sure. Please come along.
3. visit Peggy
4. visit Mr. Fox

（以下続ける）

22. 例にならい，次の語句を使って会話練習をしなさい．
　例）—May I see your folk pottery?
　　　—Sure. Here it is.
　1. Hagi-yaki
　2. your photo album
　3. your new CDs
　4. your tickets
　5. your paintings
　6. your new electronic dictionary
　7. your computer
　8. your tennis racket
　9. your golf clubs
　10. your pottery

23. 例にならい，問題22の語句を使って会話練習をしなさい．
　例）—Excuse me. May I come in?
　　　—Sure. Please do.
　　　—I'd like to ask about your folk pottery.
　　　—Go right ahead.
　　　—May I sit down?
　　　—Certainly.

24. 例にならい，問題6の語句を使って会話練習をしなさい．
　例）—I'm going to Nagoya. Would you like to come along?
　　　—Yes. That'd be very nice.
　　　—You may bring a friend, too.
　　　—Well, my friend might not want to go.

25. ⇒ Chart I.
   1. Is Bob going to play baseball? / I'm not sure. He might not. Perhaps he'll work at the bookstore.
   2. Is Harry going to work at the bookstore? / I'm not sure. He might not. Perhaps he'll go to school.

   (以下続ける)

26. ⇒ Chart V. チャートの内容によくなじむまで練習をしなさい.
   1. It's raining. What might John do? / He might go into the house, or he might stay outside, or he might stand under a tree. / What should he do? / He should go into the house.
   2. Bill is sick. What might he do? / He might go to bed, or he might see a doctor, or he might take some medicine. / What should he do? / He should see a doctor.
   3. Harry is late. What might he do? / He might take a taxi, or he might run, or he might take a bus. / What should he do? / He should take a taxi.
   4. Pete is cold. What might he do? / He might put on his coat, or he might close the window, or he might turn on the heater. / What should he do? / He should close the window.
   5. There is a burglar in the house. What might Mary do? / She might hit him with a broom, or she might hide in the closet, or she might call the police. / What should she do? / She should call the police.
   6. The dog is hungry. What might Jack do? / He might give it a bone, or he might scold it, or he might take it for a walk. / What should he do? / He should give it a bone.

27. ⇒ Chart V.
  1. It's raining. Shouldn't John go into the house? / Yes, he should.
  2. Bill's sick. Shouldn't he see a doctor? / Yes, he should.
（以下続ける）

28. 例にならい，問題6の語句を使って会話練習をしなさい．
  例) —I'd like to take a trip.
  　　—Oh? You should go to Hachijo-jima.
  　　—Why should I go there?
  　　—It's famous for its beaches.

29. ⇒ Chart I.
  1. I'd like to play baseball. / Oh, then you should go to the park. You can play there.
（7. を除いて以下続ける）

30. ⇒ Chart V.
  1. It's raining. John's trying to go into the house.
  2. Bill's sick. He's trying to see a doctor.
（以下続ける）

31. 下線の部分に適切な語句を入れなさい．
A: What time ＿＿＿＿＿ we meet?
B: How ＿＿＿＿＿ 10 o'clock?

A: Can you ＿＿＿＿＿ it later than 10?
B: Sure. How ＿＿＿＿＿ eleven o'clock?

A: Sounds good. Have you ever _____ BBQ party before?
B: Yes, of course. BBQ parties are _____ in Japan, these days.

A: Should I _____ anything to the party?
B: You might want to bring a _____ of wine.

Lesson Nine
I WONDER WHO INVENTED TELEVISION
だれがテレビを発明したのでしょう

Section I PRESENTATION CD2-13

There is a discussion about television. One person thinks it's a bad thing and the other thinks it's OK to watch TV. In the States, it is important to share your opinions and ideas. Friends share ideas and opinions.

> テレビについて議論がなされます。ある人はテレビは悪者と考えます。別の人はテレビを見ることはよいことと思っています。アメリカでは他人と意見や考えをそれぞれ分かち合うことは大切なことです。友人とは考えや意見を分かち合うものです。

Section II APPLICATION DIALOGUE CD2-14

Listen and repeat

A Do you ever watch television?

B Never. Television is like a narcotic.[1] It's habit forming.[2]

A It is, but you have to use your will power. You should just watch the worthwhile[3] programs.

B I used to watch television. I'd begin as soon as I came home from work. I'd watch it for hours.

A Who watched it with you?

B Pardon me?

A I asked who watched it with you.

B Oh, my whole family.

A And didn't your children learn anything?

B Yes, they did. They learned a lot from television. But they didn't do their homework.

テレビを見ることがありますか.

いや, 全然. テレビは麻薬みたいなものですからね. くせになりますよ.

そのとおりですね, 意志の力がいります. 見ごたえのある番組だけを見たらいいでしょう.

以前はよくテレビを見たものです. 仕事から帰るとさっそく, 見はじめましてね. 何時間でも見ていたものですよ.

どなたとごらんになったのですか.

何とおっしゃいましたか.

どなたとごらんになったのかとお尋ねしたのです.

ああ, 家族のものみんなとでした.

ところで, お子さんはテレビから何かを覚えませんでしたか.

覚えましたよ. テレビからずいぶんいろんなことを覚えました. しかし, 宿題のほうはさっぱりでしたけどね.

---

1) **narcotic** [nɑrkátik] 麻薬.
2) **It's habit forming.** くせになる.《参照》It forms bad [good] habits.（悪い[よい]習慣をつくる）
3) **worthwhile** 価値のある.《参照》It is worthwhile doing the extra work.（余分の仕事をするのはそれだけ価値がある）

A Perhaps television is more valuable than homework. I find it very educational. I wonder who invented it.

B I don't know. He was probably a good man, but his invention has turned into a Frankenstein monster.[1]

A Tell me which would be better—a world with television or a world without it.

B A world without it, of course! Television is ruining our social life. When I visit my friends, all we do is watch television.

A Perhaps that's better than useless conversation. I'd rather watch television than talk about baseball for two or three hours.

B Tell me what's wrong with baseball.

A Nothing. Except[2] talking about baseball is like a narcotic, too.

おそらく宿題よりはテレビのほうが有益でしょう。とても教育的だと思いますよ。だれが発明したのでしょうか。

知りません。たぶんいい人だったのでしょうが，彼の発明品も今ではもうフランケンシュタインの怪物ですねえ。

どちらがましでしょう——テレビのある世界とない世界とでは。

もちろん，テレビのない世界ですよ。テレビは社交生活を破壊しています。友だちを訪ねても，やることといえばもっぱらテレビを見ることですからね。

くだらない会話よりはましでしょう。私だったら2時間も3時間も野球の話をするよりは，テレビを見てたほうがましですね。

野球のどこが悪いのですか。

別に悪くないですよ。ただ野球の話も麻薬みたいなものでしょう。

---

1) **Frankenstein monster** フランケンシュタインの怪物. Shelly 夫人作の怪奇小説の中心人物. Frankenstein という若い哲学者が墓地と解剖室から得た材料で怪物を作って，これに生命を吹きこんだところ，それがものすごく凶暴で，ついに主人公の命とりになったということから，「我と我が身をほろぼすはめになる」ことをいう場合に用いられる.

2) **Nothing. Except...**「別になにもありません。ただ…」.

B Most people like baseball. Don't you ever discuss it?

A Sometimes. If I don't have anything else to talk about. Baseball is ruining society, too.

B You can't be serious.[1] Baseball is a wonderful game.

A And television is wonderful, too. Both are good, but they have to be used in moderation.[2]

| たいていの人は野球好きです．野球談義なんかしないのですか． |
| 時にはやりますよ．ほかに話すことがなければね．野球もまた社会を毒しています． |
| ご冗談でしょう．野球はすばらしい競技ですよ． |
| それならテレビだって，すばらしいですよ．どっちも悪くはないのですが，ほどほどに利用する必要がありますね． |

Section III NOTES ON CONVERSATIONAL STYLE

1. ever を伴う疑問文 'Have you ever' は過去の経験を尋ねる言い方で，'Do you ever' は習慣のあるなしや未来の可能性を尋ねる言い方です．

 a. Do you *ever* play tennis? / Yes, I do. [No, I don't.]
  （テニスをすることはありますか / はい，します［いいえ，しません］）
 b. Do you *ever* watch television? / Never.
  （テレビを見ることが，まったくありません）
 c. Don't you *ever* talk about baseball? / Sometimes.
 d. Does he *ever* come home before six o'clock? / No, he doesn't.
 e. Do they *ever* wash their car? / No, they don't.

---

1) **serious** [síriəs] 真面目な．本気の．《参照》Are you joking or serious?（きみは冗談なのか，本気なのか？）

2) **in moderation** [màdəréiʃən] 適度に，ほどよく．

2. 疑問詞を含む直接疑問文と間接疑問文
次の直接疑問文と間接疑問文の例を比較してください。疑問詞が主語の場合，その語順は変わりません．

a. Who said that?
   I know who said that.
b. Who was singing?
   He asked who was singing.
c. Who invented television?
   I wonder who invented television.
d. Which is better?
   Tell me which is better.
e. Which computer costs more?
   Ask him which computer costs more.
f. What's on the table?
   I don't know what's on the table.

3. I wonder (= I ask myself) は日本語の「〜かしら」または「〜かな」に相当します．

a. I *wonder* who came.
   （だれが来たのかしら）
b. I *wonder* who invented television.
   （テレビを発明したのはだれでしょうか）

4. What's wrong with 〜? は，日本語の「〜はどうしてだめですか」とか「〜はどうしましたか」に相当します．

a. *What's wrong with* baseball?
   （野球はどうしてだめなのですか）

b. *What's wrong with* your hand?
   （手をどうしましたか）

5. used to は現在まで継続していない過去の習慣的動作や過去のある時の状態を表わします．日本語の「前に～のことがある」「前に～でした」とか「前に～したものです」などに相当します．

a. I *used to* watch television.
   （前はテレビを見たものです）
b. He *used to* be a student here.
   （以前彼はここの生徒でした）
c. She *used to* work here.
   （彼女は前にここに勤めていました）

6. All I [you, he など] do [does] + is は，日本語の「～のすることと言えば～だけです」に相当します．

a. Jennie is very happy. *All she does is* sing.
b. John is very tired. *All he does is* sleep.
c. I'm very sick. *All I do is* take medicine.

do のかわりに他の動詞を使うこともあります．

a. *All I want is* a new pen.
   （欲しいものと言えば新しいペンだけですよ）
b. *All I need is* a little advice.
   （必要なことと言えば，ただちょっとした助言だけですよ）
c. *All he bought was* a bottle of ink.
   （買ったものと言えばただインク一瓶だけですよ）

7. would rather + 動詞は，prefer to + 動詞と同じ意味です．

    a. Would you like to play tennis? — No. I'*d rather* not. I'd *rather play* baseball.

    b. I'd like to go to the movies. — Oh, I'*d rather go* to a play.

8. find + 〜 + 形容詞は，日本語の「自分の経験で〜が〜だと思う」に相当します．

    a. Do you like television? — Yes. I *fin*d it very *interesting*.

    b. We *found* Kyoto very *beautiful*.

    c. We didn't *find* the movie *interesting*.

9. more + 形容詞 + **than**　　長い形容詞の比較形．

    a. Which is more interesting—this book or that one? / That one is *more interesting than* this one.

    b. The camera is *more expensive than* the pen.

10. would + 動詞は，しばしば過去の不規則な習慣を表わします．

    a. I used to study French. I'*d study* for two hours every day.

    b. He used to be a police officer. He'*d work* very hard.

Section IV PRONUNCIATION DRILL CD2-15

1. Pronunciation of [f] [v] **and** [b]　([f] [v] および [b] の発音)　まず上前歯に下唇を軽くあてます．次に唇と歯の間から強く息を吹き出してごらんなさい．それが [f] の音です．こんどは [f] と同じやり方で，有声音を出してごらんなさい．それが [v] の音です．[b] は日本語の[バ]の 'b' の音と同じです．

Listen and repeat

1. face [feis]   vase [veis]   base [beis]
2. fail [feil]   veil [veil]   bale [beil]
3. fat [fæt]   vat [væt]   bat [bæt]
4. fend [fend] vend [vend] bend [bend]
5. fox [fɑks]   vox [vɑks]   box [bɑks]

Exercise: 次の下線部に上記の語を入れて言いなさい．

What does _____ mean?

▎**2. Pronunciation of [f] and [h]** ([f] と [h] の発音)　ローマ字では [フ] を fu と書きますが，日本語では [f] の音は使いません．[フ] と言ってごらんなさい．唇と唇の間から息が出てゆくでしょう．英語の [f] は上前歯と下唇の間の狭いすきまから息が出るときの音です．

Listen and repeat

1. who'd [huːd]   food [fuːd]
2. who'll [huːl]   fool [fuːl]
3. hoar [hɔr]   four [fɔr]
4. hall [hɔll]   fall [fɔl]
5. hold [hould]   fold [fould]
6. hive [haiv]   five [faiv]
7. height [hait] fight [fait]

Section V PATTERN USAGE DRILL CD2-16

Listen and repeat

1. ⇒ Chart I.

1. Do you ever play baseball? / Yes, I do. Does Bob ever play

baseball? / No, he doesn't.

（以下続ける）

2. ⇒ Chart I.
1. Do you ever play baseball? / No. Not now. But I used to play baseball.

（以下続ける）

3. 例にならい，次の語句を使って問いと答を言いなさい．
例) play chess / Do you ever play chess now? / No. I never play chess now. But I used to play last year.
1. watch baseball
2. listen to jazz
3. talk about baseball
4. talk about tennis
5. collect stamps
6. study French
7. listen to classical music
8. play the piano
9. play soccer
10. go fishing

4. 例にならい，問いと答を言いなさい(問いには ever を使うこと)．
例) Do you ever eat Japanese food? / Yes, I do. Do you ever eat Chinese food? / No, I don't.

5. 例にならい，問題 3 の語句を使って問いと答を言いなさい．
例) play chess / Do you like to play chess? / No, not now. / Did you use to like to play chess? / Yes, I did.

6. 例にならい，次の語句を使って会話練習をしなさい．
例) —Do you ever watch television?
—No, not now. But I used to watch it.
—Did you watch it very much?

—Yes. I'd watch it two or three hours every day.
—Who watched it with you?
—Pardon me?
—I asked who watched it with you.
—Oh, my friends.

1. play tennis
2. practice judo
3. listen to jazz
4. sing songs
5. play chess
6. watch baseball on television
7. play *shogi*
8. talk about tennis
9. watch sumo
10. talk about politics

7. ⇒ Chart I.
   1. Do you know who's playing baseball? / No. I don't know who's playing baseball.

（以下続ける）

8. ⇒ Chart III.
   1. Who went to Oshima? / Pardon me? I couldn't hear you. / I asked who went to Oshima. / I don't know. I wonder who went to Oshima, too.

（以下続ける）

9. 例にならい，問題 3 の語句を使って問いと答を言いなさい．
   例）play chess / I wonder who's going to play chess. / I don't know. Shall I ask someone who's going to play? / Yes. Please ask someone who's going to play.

10. ⇒ Chart I.
　1. Can you tell me who's playing baseball? / Yes, I'll be glad to. Bob is.
（以下続ける）

11. ⇒ Chart III.
　1. What did you ask Bill? / I asked him who went to Oshima.

12. ⇒ Chart IV.
　1. I wonder who's singing. Do you know? / No. I don't know who's singing.
（以下続ける）

13. ⇒ Chart V.
　1. John wants to know who went inside. / All right. I'll tell him who went inside.
　I want to know who stayed outside. / All right. I'll tell you who stayed outside.
　Do you want to know who stood under a tree? / Yes. I want to know who stood under a tree.
（以下続ける）

14. ⇒ Chart V.
　1. Do you know who should go into the house? / No, I don't. I don't know who should go into the house.
　Do you know who should stay outside? / No, I don't. I don't know who should stay outside.
　Do you know who should stand under a tree? / No, I don't. I don't know who should stand under a tree.

（以下続ける）

15. ⇒ Chart I.
1. I wonder which is better—playing baseball or working at the bookstore. / Oh, playing baseball is better than working at the bookstore.
2. I wonder which is more interesting—working at the bookstore or going to school. / Oh, working at the bookstore is more interesting than going to school.
3. more fun
4. better
5. better
6. more important
7. better
8. more interesting
9. more fun

16. 例にならい，次の語句を使って対話を完成しなさい．
例) I wonder which is more valuable—this gold watch or this silver watch. / Oh, the gold watch is more valuable than the silver one is.
1. interesting / this educational program / this sports program
2. useful / this dictionary / that dictionary
3. delicious / these apples / those apples
4. good / the French movie / the American movie
5. useful / the English class / the French class
6. habit forming / television / the radio
7. worthwhile / television programs / movies
8. difficult / learning Spanish / learning Greek
9. interesting / collecting pottery / collecting stamps

10. small / Kobe / Kyoto

17. ⇒ Chart II.
   1. Do you want a pen and some paper? / No. I don't want both. All I want is a pen.

（以下続ける）

18. ⇒ Chart IV.
   1. All Jennie does is sing. I wonder why. / Well, she's very happy.
   2. All Jimmy does is cry. I wonder why. / Well, he's very sad.

19. ⇒ Chart IV.
   1. All Jennie used to do was sing. / Yes. But now she never sings.
   2. All Jimmy used to do was cry. / Yes. But now he never cries.

（以下続ける）

20. 例にならい，斜字体の部分に問題3の語句を使って会話練習をしなさい．
   例）—Are you going to be busy this afternoon?
   　　—No. All I have to do is write a letter.
   　　—Shall we *go to the movies*, then?
   　　—All right. Let's do that.

21. 例にならい，斜字体の部分に問題6の語句を使って会話練習をしなさい．
   例）—Shall we visit John this afternoon?
   　　—No, let's not.
   　　—Oh? Why not?
   　　—He's not very interesting. All he wants to do is *play chess*.

22. ⇒ Chart I.
1. I don't like to play baseball. / Oh? What's wrong with playing baseball? / Nothing. Except I don't find it very interesting.
（以下続ける）

23. 例にならい，問題16の語句を使って対話を完成しなさい．
例) Which did you find more interesting—the movie or the book? / Oh, I found the movie more interesting. / Oh? What was wrong with the book? / Well, I'm not sure.

24. ⇒ Chart I.
1. What does Bob do on Sundays? / All he does is play baseball.
2. What does Harry do on Mondays? / All he does is work at the bookstore.
（以下続ける）

25. ⇒ Chart IV.
1. I met Jennie the other day. / Oh? What did you think of her? / Well, I found her very happy. All she did was sing.
（以下続ける）

26. ⇒ Chart I.
1. Shall we play baseball or go to the bookstore? / I'd rather play baseball.
2. Shall we go to the bookstore or go to school? / I'd rather go to the bookstore.
（以下続ける）

27. ⇒ Chart III.
1. Would you rather go to Oshima than go to the zoo? / No. I'd rather go to the zoo.
2. Would you rather go to the zoo than visit Peggy? / No. I'd rather visit Peggy.

（以下続ける）

28. 例にならい，問題 3 の語句を使って問いと答を言いなさい．
例) Would you like to play *shogi*? / No, thanks. I'd rather play chess.

29. 例にならい，問題 16 の語句を使って言い換えなさい．
例) Which did you find more interesting—the movie or the book? / Well, both were interesting. I found them both interesting.

30. ⇒ Chart I.
1. Have you ever played baseball? / Yes. I used to play. I'd play every Sunday.
2. Have you ever worked at the bookstore? / Yes. I used to work there. I'd work there every Monday.

（以下続ける）

31. 次の話を読み，問いに答えなさい．

Bill doesn't like television now. He thinks it's like a narcotic. It's habit forming. He used to watch television every day. He'd begin as soon as he came home from work. His whole family would watch it with him. His children learned a lot from television. But they didn't do their homework. When Bill visits his friends, all he does is watch television. Bill says, "Television is ruining our social life. A world without television would be better than a world with it."

   1. What does Bill think of television now?
   2. Why doesn't he watch it now?
   3. Why is television like a narcotic?
   4. Bill used to watch television. When would he begin each day?
   5. Does Bill have any children?
   6. How many children does Bill have?
   7. Did Bill's children learn anything from television?
   8. Why is television ruining our social life?
   9. Which does Bill prefer—a world with or without television?
   10. Which do you prefer? Explain.

32. 下線の部分に適切な語句を入れなさい.

A: _____ is the new teacher at your school?
B: I don't know, but he _____ to teach in Chicago.

A: I wonder what _____ a teacher he is.
B: I hope he is more _____ than our last teacher.

A: Yes. I agree. I _____ our last teacher very boring.
B: Yes. All he _____ was give lectures and tests.

A: What's wrong _____ taking tests?
B: I would _____ use class time for discussion.

Lesson Ten

I WONDER WHAT HE BOUGHT
彼は何を買ったのでしょう

Section I PRESENTATION CD2-17

Three people are going to a football game. They plan to meet at the stadium. They are wondering if they will meet. One person doesn't understand football very well. In America, "football" means American football not soccer. In the rest of the world, "football" means soccer.

3人の人がフットボールの試合の観戦を行おうとしています．競技場で落ち合う予定です．みんな待ち合わせがうまくいくか気にしています．フットボールがよくわからない人もいます．アメリカでは「フットボール」と言えば,「アメリカンフットボール」であって，サッカーではありません．アメリカ以外の世界では「フットボール」はサッカーのことです．

Section II APPLICATION DIALOGUE CD2-18

Listen and repeat

A	What time is it now?	今，何時かしら？
B	Pardon me?	何だって？
A	I asked you what time it is now.	今，何時かって聞いてるのよ．
B	Oh, it's three-fifteen. We have to hurry.	ああそうか．3時15分だよ．急がなくちゃ．
A	Do you know where we're going to meet George?	ジョージとどこで会うのか知ってるの？
B	Yes. In front of the stadium—at the main gate.	ああ，スタジアムの前さ——正門のとこだよ．
A	I wonder what kind of tickets he bought.	彼はどんな席の切符を買ったのかしら．
B	Well, you know George.[1] He probably bought the cheapest ones.	そりゃ，ジョージのことだからね．いちばん安いのを買っただろうさ．
A	Do you know how much reserved seats are?	指定席はいくらか知ってる？
B	I think they're ten-fifty.[2]	10ドル50セントだと思う．
A	That's awfully expensive. George probably bought general admission tickets.[3]	すごく高いわね．ジョージはたぶん，自由席の切符を買ったんじゃないかしら．

---

1) **You know George.** = You know what sort of a person George is. ジョージの人柄を知っているだろう．

2) **ten-fifty** = ten dollars and fifty cents (each).

3) **general admission tickets** 自由席の切符．

Lesson Ten

B I wonder why you want to come with us. I thought you didn't like football.

A I don't. But I want you and George to teach me something about it.

B Well, please don't ask me to explain the game. I'm not going to tutor you in football.

A All right. I'll ask George to explain it.

B Well, here's the main gate. I don't see George.

A I wonder where he is. He's usually on time.

B Yes. But we're a little late. You know how much George likes football. Maybe he's already gone in.

A I hope not. He's got the tickets, and I didn't bring any money with me.

B Oh, there he is. Over there.

A I can't see him. Where is he?

B Right there. See. He's jumping up and down and waving. He wants us to hurry.

A Oh, yes. I see him now.

B Let's hurry. It's almost game time.

君は何だってぼくらといっしょに来る気になったんじゃない？ フットボールは好きじゃないと思っていたんだけど.

好きじゃないわ. だけど, あなたとジョージにフットボールのことを少し教えてもらおうと思ったの.

そうだとしても, ぼくにゲームの説明してくれって言わないでくれよ. フットボールの個人教授をするつもりはないよ.

いいわ, 説明はジョージに頼むから.

さあ, 正門へ来たぞ. ジョージの姿が見えないね.

どこにいるのかしら. いつも時間には正確なんだけど.

うん. だけどぼくたちが少し遅れたからな. ジョージのフットボール好きがどんなか知ってるだろう. もう中へはいってしまったのかもしれないよ.

そうでないといいけど. 切符はあの人が持ってるんだし, それに私はお金を持ってこなかったもの.

ああ, あそこにいるよ. 向こうに.

私には見えないけど. どこにいるの.

あそこだよ. ほら！ ピョンピョン跳んで手を振ってるよ. 急いでくれってさ.

ああ, ほんと. やっとわかったわ.

急ごうよ. そろそろ試合の始まる時間だ.

Section III NOTES ON CONVERSATIONAL STYLE

▥ **1. 疑問詞を含む間接疑問**　疑問詞を含む場合の直接疑問文と間接疑問文の各例文を比較しましょう．疑問詞が主語ではない場合，間接疑問文では語順が普通の文のようになります．

   a. *What* time is it now?

   　 I asked you *what* time it is now.

   b. *How* much are reserved seats?

   　 Do you know *how* much reserved seats are?

   c. *Where* are we going to meet George?

   　 Do you know *where* we're going to meet George?

   d. *What* kind of tickets did he buy?

   　 I wonder *what* kind of tickets he bought.

   e. *Why* do you want to come with us?

   　 I wonder *why* you want to come with us.

▥ **2.** '**want** [**ask, tell** など] + **you** [**him, the man** など] + **to** + 動詞の原形' は，日本語の「君に[だれかに]～をしてもらいたい[たのむ，話す]」に相当します．

   a. I *want him to* study harder.

   　 （私は彼にもっと勉強してもらいたいと思っています）

   b. I *asked him to* explain the game.

   　 （ゲームの説明をするように彼に頼みました）

   c. They *told us to* come early.

   　 （早く来るように彼らは私たちに言った）

   d. I'*d like you to* play the piano.

   　 （あなたにピアノをひいていただきたいのです）

Lesson Ten

3. have got は have と同じ意味に使うことがあります.

 a. *Have* you *got* a lighter? / Yes, I have.
 b. He *hasn't got* any tickets.
 c. *Haven't* they *got* a car? / No, they haven't.
  cf. Do you have a car? / Yes, I do.

Section IV PRONUNCIATION DRILL CD2-19

1. Pronunciation of [ʃ] and [s] ([ʃ] と [s] の発音)　日本語の「します」を発音してごらんなさい.「し」が大した摩擦もなく, ごく軽いことに注意してください. 英語の音 [ʃ] を発音するには, 唇をいくぶん丸くし, 日本語の「し」を言う普通の位置より突き出し気味にするのです. [ʃ] と発音してごらんなさい.

Listen and repeat

 sheep [ʃi:p]   shut [ʃʌt]
 ship [ʃip]   shot [ʃɑt]
 shale [ʃeil]   shoe [ʃu:]
 sham [ʃæm]   should [ʃud]

注意: 接尾辞 -tion や -shion はたいていの場合 [ʃən] と発音します. [ʃn] と発音することもあります.

 nation [néiʃən] fashion [fǽʃən]
 position [pəzíʃən] collection [kəlékʃən]
 notion [nóuʃən] sensation [senséiʃən]
 motion [móuʃən] cushion [kúʃən]

Listen and repeat

 ship [ʃip]   sip [sip]

shore [ʃɔr]　　　sore [sɔr]
shoe [ʃuː]　　　sue [suː]
mush [mʌʃ]　　　muss [mʌs]
gushed [gʌʃt]　　gust [gʌst]

Exercise: 次の＿＿に上記の語を入れて練習しなさい.
Do you remember whether he said ＿＿＿ or ＿＿＿?

2. Review dialogue（復習用対話）

—[helou　hau ɑr juː]
—[fain θæŋks　hau ɚ juː]
—[kudnt biː betɚ　hwɑt əv jə bin duːiŋ leitli]
—[ou stʌdiŋ ə litl iŋgliʃ]
—[ai noutis jɚ prənʌnsieiʃənz impruːvd ə lɑt]
—[θæŋks bət ai stil kænt distiŋgwiʃ bitwiːn biːt n bit]
—[jes iː n i ɑr difikəlt ɔlrait bət hau əbaut el n ɑr]
—[mai tiːtʃɚ sez ai prənauns əm priti wel]
—[ðæts kwait n əkɑmpliʃmənt]
—[ai fiːl praud əv it maiself]

— Hello. How are you?
— Fine, thanks. How are you?
— Couldn't be better. What have you been doing lately?
— Oh studying a little English.
— I notice your pronunciations improved a lot.
— Thanks, but I still can't distinguish between beet and bit.
— Yes, i: and i are difficult all right, but how about l and r?
— My teacher says I pronounce them pretty well.
— That's quite an accomplishment.
— I feel proud of it myself.

Lesson Ten

Section V PATTERN USAGE DRILL CD2-20

Listen and repeat

1. ⇒ Chart I.

  1. Where do you play baseball? / Pardon me? I couldn't hear what you said. / I asked where you play baseball. / Oh, I play in the park.

  （以下続ける）

2. ⇒ Chart III.

  1. Did Bill go to Oshima? / I don't know where he went.
  2. Did Sachiko go to the zoo? / I don't know where she went.

  （以下続ける）

3. ⇒ Chart III.

  1. Bill went to Oshima. / Yes, I know. I wonder how he went. Did he go by boat? / I don't know how he went.

  （以下続ける）

4. ⇒ Chart III.

  1. Bill went to Oshima. / Yes, I know. Tell me why he went there. / I don't know why he went there.

  （以下続ける）

5. ⇒ Chart IV.

  1. Why does Jennie sing every day? / I don't know. I wonder why she sings every day, too.

  （以下続ける）

6. ⇒ Chart I.
1. How long have Bob and Dick been playing baseball? / I don't know. Why don't you ask them how long they've been playing? / All right. I will.

(以下続ける)

7. ⇒ Chart V.
1. It's raining. I wonder what John should do. / He should go into the house. Isn't that what he should do? / Yes, it is.

8. 例にならい，次の疑問文の文頭に I wonder を置いて言い換えなさい．
例) When did you come to Japan? / I wonder when you came to Japan.
1. What time is it now?
2. Where are we going to meet Mary?
3. How much are general admission tickets?
4. What school do you go to?
5. How long do we have to wait here?
6. Why don't you like football?
7. Why didn't he bring any money with him?
8. Who went to Mexico with George?
9. When does he have to go home?
10. What kind of food do you like?

9. 例にならい，問題 8 の疑問文の前に Please tell me を置いて言い換えなさい．
例) When did you come to Japan? / Please tell me when you came to Japan.

10. 例にならい，問題 8 の疑問文を言い換え，否定で答えなさい．
例）When did you come to Japan? / Does anyone know when you came to Japan? / No. No one knows when I came to Japan.

11. 例にならい，問題 8 の各文を使って会話練習をしなさい．
例）—When did you come to Japan?
—Pardon me? I couldn't hear what you said.
—I asked when you came to Japan.
—Oh, I came here in 2005.

12. 例にならい，次の各疑問文から始めて対話を完成しなさい．
例）Who came here tonight? / Pardon me? I couldn't hear what you said. / Oh, I was just wondering who came here tonight. / Oh, I don't know who came here tonight.
1. When did she get home?
2. Who did he see downtown?
3. Who saw them downtown?
4. Why don't they like John?
5. Why is television like a narcotic?
6. Why was John late?
7. Who won't explain the game?
8. Who asked George to explain the game?
9. Where's George?
10. Where did she see him?

13. 例にならい，問題 12 の疑問文の前に Don't tell anyone を置き，その答も言いなさい．
例）Who came here tonight? / Don't tell anyone who came here

tonight. / Oh? Why shouldn't I tell anyone who came here tonight? / Because I don't want you to.

14. ⇒ Chart I.
   1. What do you want to do? / I want to play baseball. / What do you want me to do? / I want you to play, too.

（以下続ける）

15. ⇒ Chart III.
   1. I'd like to go to Oshima. / Oh? Do you want to go alone? / No. I'd like Bill to go, too.

（以下続ける）

16. ⇒ Chart I.
   1. What did you tell Bob to do? / I told him to play baseball.

（以下続ける）

17. ⇒ Chart II.
   1. I'll get a pen. / Oh? What would you like me to get? / I'd like you to get some paper.

（以下続ける）

18. 例にならい，次の語句を使って言いなさい．
   例）study English / I want you to study English.
   1. tutor me in English
   2. tell me the time
   3. buy general admission tickets
   4. ask how much reserved seats are
   5. teach me something about soccer

6. explain English sentences
7. tell me why you're late
8. bring some money
9. explain why you don't like football
10. explain something about the United States

19. 例にならい，問題 18 の語句の前に I didn't ask him を置いて言い換えなさい．

例) study English / I didn't ask him to study English.

20. ⇒ Chart II.
1. Have you got a pen? / Yes, I have. Do you have some paper? / Yes, I do.

（以下続ける）

21. 例にならい，Have you got 〜? の疑問文を作りなさい．
例) Have you got a lighter? / Yes. Here you are. / Thanks. / You're welcome.
Have you got a piece of gum? / Yes. Here you are. / Thanks. / You're welcome.

22. 例にならい，次の語句を使って会話練習をしなさい．
例) —Have you got any money?
—No. I didn't bring any money with me.
—That's all right. I brought some with me.

—Have you got a pen?
—No. I didn't bring a pen with me.
—That's all right. I brought one with me.

1. a camera
2. any film
3. any tickets
4. any gum
5. a handkerchief
6. a knife
7. any yen
8. any dollars
9. any sandwiches
10. any juice
11. any vitamin pills
12. a CD player

23. 例にならい，問題22の語句を使って会話練習をしなさい．
例) —I'm going out now.
　　—O.K. I want you to take some money with you.
　　—All right. I'll do that.
　　—I want you to be careful, too.
　　—Don't worry. I will.

24. ⇒ Chart III.
1. Is Bill still here? / No. He's already gone to Oshima.
（以下続ける）

25. 下線の部分に適切な語句を入れなさい．
A: What time is it ＿＿＿＿＿?
B: I don't know. I ＿＿＿＿＿ a watch.

A: I'd ＿＿＿＿＿ know what time it is. I have an appointment.
B: Why don't you ＿＿＿＿＿ that shop, they have a clock?

A: I wonder ＿＿＿＿＿ they have a clock.
B: Of course, they ＿＿＿＿＿.

A: I _____ the man in the shop, but he doesn't know the time.
B: What? They don't have a clock? And he _____ a watch?

KENKYUSHA

〈検印省略〉

アメリカ口語教本・入門用（最新改訂版）
SPOKEN AMERICAN ENGLISH (*Introductory Course*)

1959 年 12 月 20 日	初 版 発 行
1962 年 1 月 25 日	改訂新版発行
1972 年 11 月 26 日	三 訂 版 発 行
1984 年 4 月 5 日	新 訂 版 発 行
2006 年 10 月 20 日	最新改訂版発行
2025 年 2 月 28 日	20 刷 発 行

著　者　W. L. クラーク
発行者　吉　田　尚　志
印刷所　TOPPAN クロレ株式会社

発行所　株式会社　研　究　社

〒102-8152
東京都千代田区富士見 2-11-3
電話 （編集）03(3288)7711(代)
　　 （営業）03(3288)7777(代)
振替　00150-9-26710

Printed in Japan / ISBN978-4-327-44087-9　C1082
https://www.kenkyusha.co.jp/

1
2
3
4
5
6
7
8
9

CH

1.
2.
3.
4.
5.
6.
7.
8.
9.

CHA

1. H
2. H
3. H
4. H
5. H
   v
6. H
7. H
   v
8. H
   b
9. H